D1406775

Hot Honey
COOKBOOK

Hot Honey
COOKBOOK

*60 Recipes to Infuse Sweet Heat
into Your Favorite Foods*

Ames Russell of AR's Hot Southern Honey
with Sara Quessenberry

ROCK
POINT

Brimming with creative inspiration, how-to projects, and useful information to enrich your everyday life, quarto.com is a favorite destination for those pursuing their interests and passions.

© 2022 by Quarto Publishing Group USA Inc.

First published in 2022 by Rock Point, an imprint of The Quarto Group, 142 West 36th Street, 4th Floor, New York, NY 10018, USA
T (212) 779-4972 F (212) 779-6058 www.Quarto.com

All rights reserved. No part of this book may be reproduced in any form without written permission of the copyright owners. All images in this book have been reproduced with the knowledge and prior consent of the artists concerned, and no responsibility is accepted by producer, publisher, or printer for any infringement of copyright or otherwise, arising from the contents of this publication. Every effort has been made to ensure the credits accurately comply with information supplied. We apologize for any inaccuracies that may have occurred and will resolve inaccurate or missing information in a subsequent reprinting of the book.

Rock Point titles are also available at discount for retail, wholesale, promotional and bulk purchase. For details, contact the Special Sales Manager by email at specialsales@quarto.com or by mail at The Quarto Group, Attn: Special Sales Manager, 100 Cummings Center Suite, 265D, Beverly, MA 01915, USA.

10 9 8 7 6 5 4 3 2 1

ISBN: 978-1-63106-848-5

Library of Congress Control Number: 2022930434

Publisher: Rage Kindelsperger
Creative Director: Laura Drew
Managing Editor: Cara Donaldson
Senior Editor: Erin Canning
Cover Design: Marisa Kwek
Page Layout: Silverglass
Photography: Chelsea Chorpenning: cover and pages 2, 13, 16, 18, 26, 29, 34, 37, 38, 41, 47, 54, 56, 59, 65, 68, 75, 81, 86, 89, 94, 110, 119, 124, 126, 129, 132, 134

Erik Leskovar (Food Styling): pages 2, 13, 16, 18, 26, 29, 34, 38, 41, 47, 54, 56, 59, 65, 68, 75, 81, 86, 89, 94, 110, 119, 124, 126, 129, 132, 134

Sarah Zivic (Food Styling): Cover and page 37

Jordan Hanna (Photography) and Helen Russell (Food Styling): pages 50, 63, 114

All other images © Shutterstock

Printed in China

For people everywhere looking for fun and healthy ways to flavor their food.

And a special thanks to my family, friends, and fans!

contents

introduction

These days, it seems like every time you go grocery shopping, there's a new condiment fighting for that precious shelf space—often something that promises to enhance your favorite foods with some spice and heat. Although most of these condiments have a short shelf life, a select few rise to the top and earn a permanent spot. Sriracha sauce is a good example of a condiment that started out as a trend and is now ubiquitous, inspiring countless chili-sauce upstarts, along with the hunt for other classic condiments available in Asian markets. And the same can be said for hot honey.

Hot honey has been around for the last decade but is now starting to feel like it has legs and is everywhere, including on the menus of fast-food chains. This honey infused with the heat of chili peppers stands out from other spicy, hot condiments not only because of its sweet heat, but also its versatility—it works with savory-and-sweet foods and drinks. It's also a flavor combination we are familiar with, especially if you ever indulged in candies like Atomic Fireballs and Red Hots.

Always great for drizzling on fried chicken, pizza, tacos, baked Brie, ice cream, and yogurt, hot honey also can be used in other ways, and this cookbook is here to answer the first question people always ask me: How do you use hot honey? So, get ready to make these sixty easy and delicious Southern-, Asian-, and Latin-inspired recipes that use hot honey for marinades, glazes, dressings, sauces, drizzling, and so much more!

Opposite: Ames Russell, founder of AR's Hot Southern Honey

The Origin of AR's Hot Southern Honey

I always loved drizzling honey on my fried chicken, and at some point, I started adding hot sauce or red pepper flakes to the honey to give that sweetness a spicy kick. One evening it occurred to me that this could be a product—hot honey! My grandfather, who was also named Ames, had kept bees and always had a honeycomb on the kitchen table, so I felt that this was my calling. I didn't know much about honey or chili peppers, so I did a lot of research on both topics. I started experimenting by infusing different honeys with different peppers and came up with a combination everyone in my family loved. It became a household condiment and was always on hand.

In 2015, my wife, Carrie, and I gifted one hundred bottles of my hot honey as holiday gifts. A couple months later, I started receiving calls from those whom I had gifted the hot honey: "We loved your hot honey!" "We put it on everything!" "Where can we get more?" I was amazed by my family and friends' reactions to and interest in my hot honey. As a serial entrepreneur, I was intrigued by the possibility of turning this interest into a marketable product, so I researched the necessary steps to bring CPG (consumer product goods) to market.

My first task was to prove that I could turn the concept into a marketable product. Much of my career has been spent marketing products to the retail trade (in the sporting goods business), so I knew the landscape and dynamics of retail and was comfortable in it. My proof of concept was not only to sell the product and get it placed on a shelf, but once it was on a shelf, it needed to sell without me standing in the aisle and pointing to it. Most importantly, retailers had to reorder it.

To begin, I needed to gain the necessary process approvals and inspections to produce my first batch to market to retail. I went through the required steps and was ready to go into the kitchen, but I needed a lot of honey, gallons of it, and no local stores sold that much. I called local honey producers, but no one had the amount I needed, and I didn't want to aggregate a gallon here and a gallon there; I wanted the total amount from one place. There was a well-known local beer brewer that marketed a honey beer, so I assumed they had a supplier who could deliver large quantities of honey. I called them and was referred to a supplier in the Shenandoah Valley of Virginia, who I have been working with since then.

For weeks after I produced that first batch of hot honey in a rented commercial kitchen (thank you, Louise!), I would visit stores and introduce my product, after a day's work at my full-time job. As expected, I was able to get my product placed on shelves, but when retailers started calling for reorders, I had proved my concept that I could commercialize the interest in my hot honey from family and friends.

Since I started selling my original hot honey, AR's Hot Southern Honey has added three more honey products inspired by feedback from customers and retailers (an even spicier hot honey and wildflower and clover honeys without heat), along with a collaboration with another Virginia producer, Ironclad Distillery, in Newport News (a bourbon barrel-aged hot honey). After I developed the fifth product, I realized two things: the appeal of my products was based on three concepts, all of which were (and are) trending—hot, Southern, honey—and ultimately to grow a CPG company, I needed a brand family of products. To grow the brand family beyond honey and still incorporate these three concepts, I introduced a peach hot sauce made with honey and a spicy honey peanut butter.

Initially, my focus for distribution was to retail, until I had my first setback: a customer decided to stop carrying my product because other retailers in town were doing so. As I walked out of the store, I received a message from a friend that a pizza shop across the street from where I was at that moment was featuring my honey on a pizza. One door closes and another opens! This changed my focus to also include distribution to the food-service industry. There are many restaurants who incorporate our products into menu items, as well as breweries, distilleries, bakeries, and others who use our honeys as ingredients in their products.

As homage to a handful of early adopters and influencers of my brand, a recipe is included in each section showing how they best enjoy our hot honey, and you can learn more about each contributor on page 143.

The Main Ingredient

Most of the recipes call for either the mild or hot version of hot honey, depending on your heat preference, with our Peach Hot Sauce and Bourbon Barrel Aged Hot-Hot Southern Honey making appearances in a couple of recipes.

Here's a little more information about our award-winning hot honeys that stand out from others on the market for the quality of the honey and peppers, our proprietary infusion process, and all-natural ingredients (no artificial sugar, additives, preservatives, vinegar, or extracts). They are also gluten-free and paleo-friendly.

AR's Hot-Mild Southern Honey

Our original, best-selling hot honey is made with a blend of 100 percent pure sweet clover and wildflower honeys and red chili peppers. It starts off sweet and then packs a fun sting of heat at the end. This mild-hot honey falls right in the middle of the spiciness scale; it's not too hot and not too sweet.

AR's Hot-Hot Southern Honey

The fourth product we developed based on consistent feedback from customers, this hot-hot honey is made with a blend of 100 percent pure sweet clover and wildflower honeys and habanero peppers. The heat intensity is much more robust than the mild version because of the hot, smoky kick of the habaneros, and instead of a spicy sting at the end, the heat comes sooner and lingers longer.

breakfast

Everything Biscuits

25 minutes *Makes 8 biscuits*

2 cups (240 g) all-purpose flour, plus more for work surface

1 tablespoon baking powder

¼ teaspoon baking soda

¾ teaspoon kosher salt

6 tablespoons cold unsalted butter, cut into small pieces, plus more for serving

1 cup (240 ml) cold buttermilk

1 tablespoon AR's Hot Southern Honey (mild or hot), plus more for serving

1 tablespoon everything seasoning

1. Preheat the oven to 450°F (230°C; gas mark 8).

2. In a medium bowl, whisk together the flour, baking powder, baking soda, and salt.

3. Add the butter. Working quickly so that the butter doesn't soften, use a pastry cutter or your fingertips to cut the butter into pea-size pieces.

4. Pour in the buttermilk and, using a fork, stir until the dough just comes together. The dough will be a little sticky.

5. Turn the dough out onto a floured work surface and shape into a 1-inch-thick (2.5 cm) rectangle. Fold it into thirds, folding each short end toward the middle. Gently flatten the rectangle and repeat the folding process one more time. Shape into a 1-inch-thick (2.5 cm) disk.

6. Using a 2½-inch (6 cm) round cutter or glass to cut the biscuits, push straight down through the dough without turning the cutter. Reshape and cut the scraps as necessary.

7. Place the biscuits in a cast-iron skillet or on a parchment paper–lined sheet pan, spacing them about ½ inch (1 cm) apart. Drizzle the tops with the hot honey and sprinkle with the everything seasoning.

8. Bake for 15 to 20 minutes, until golden brown.

9. Serve immediately with more butter and hot honey.

Nashville Fried Chicken Breakfast Tacos

CONTRIBUTED BY MIKE LEDESMA

40 minutes, plus overnight marinating time *Serves 2*

4 large eggs, divided

1 cup (240 ml) buttermilk

2 boneless, skinless chicken thighs or breasts

1 cup (240 ml) peanut or vegetable oil, for frying

1 cup (112 g) chicken breader

¾ cup (90 g) all-purpose flour

2 tablespoons cornstarch

1 tablespoon garlic powder

1 tablespoon cayenne pepper

1 teaspoon salt, plus more to taste

¼ teaspoon freshly ground black pepper, plus more to taste

1 tablespoon onion powder

1 teaspoon paprika

3 tablespoons AR's Hot Southern Honey (mild or hot), for drizzling

2 tablespoons oil of choice, for scrambling eggs

¼ cup (28 g) shredded Chihuahua cheese, plus more for serving

1 scallion, chopped, plus more for serving

1 teaspoon chopped cilantro, plus more for serving

6 corn tortillas

½ avocado, sliced, for serving (optional)

1. In a medium bowl, mix one of the eggs with the buttermilk. Add the chicken to the bowl, cover, and marinate in the refrigerator overnight.

2. Add the 1 cup (240 ml peanut oil) to a large heavy-bottomed skillet and heat over medium-high heat to 350°F (175°C; gas mark 4). Line a plate with two paper towels and set aside.

3. Place the chicken breader in a medium shallow bowl and mix with the flour, cornstarch, garlic powder, cayenne, salt, pepper, onion powder, and paprika. Remove the chicken from the marinade and dredge it in the breader mixture. Gently drop the chicken into the skillet and fry until golden brown or an instant-read thermometer inserted into the center reads 165°F (74°C). Transfer to the prepared plate.

4. Once the chicken is cool enough to handle, cut it into smaller pieces, then drizzle with the 3 tablespoons hot honey.

5. Whisk the remaining three eggs in a small bowl for scrambled eggs. In a small skillet, heat the 2 tablespoons oil over medium heat, then add the eggs and cook, folding and stirring occasionally to prevent them from sticking to the pan, until desired firmness. Season with salt and pepper, then stir in the cheese, scallions, and cilantro.

6. Warm the tortillas in an oven or toaster oven.

7. To assemble the tacos, lay some scrambled egg topped with chicken in each tortilla and garnish with the avocado (if using), cheese, scallions, and cilantro.

Cornmeal Blueberry Brown Butter Muffins

40 minutes *Makes 12 muffins*

Nonstick vegetable oil cooking spray, for the pan

6 tablespoons unsalted butter

¾ cup (150 g) sugar

¼ cup (85 g) AR's Hot Southern Honey (mild)

1 large egg

½ cup (115 g) Greek yogurt

1 teaspoon grated lemon zest

1¼ cups (150 g) all-purpose flour

½ cup (70 g) finely ground cornmeal

1 teaspoon baking powder

¼ teaspoon baking soda

¾ teaspoon kosher salt

1¼ cups (155 g) fresh or frozen blueberries

1. Preheat the oven to 350°F (175°C; gas mark 4). Spray a 12-cup muffin pan (or two 6-cup muffin pans) with cooking spray. Set aside.

2. Melt the butter in a small skillet over medium heat. Once it is melted, swirl the skillet for 3 to 4 minutes, constantly, until the milk solids start to turn a light golden brown (be careful; they can burn quickly). Remove from the heat and let cool for a few minutes.

3. In a large bowl, whisk together the sugar, hot honey, egg, yogurt, and lemon zest. Whisk in the brown butter.

4. In a medium bowl, whisk together the flour, cornmeal, baking powder, baking soda, and salt.

5. Gently stir in the dry ingredients to the wet ingredients. Fold in the blueberries.

6. Dividing evenly, spoon the batter into the prepared muffin cups.

7. Bake for 18 to 20 minutes, until springy to the touch and a toothpick inserted in the middle comes out with a few moist crumbs attached.

8. Let cool for 15 minutes before unmolding.

Poached Eggs and Honey Ham on English Muffins

25 minutes *Serves 4*

½ teaspoon white wine vinegar

4 English muffins

Salted butter, for spreading

2 ham steaks, ¼ inch (6 mm) thick

8 large eggs

AR's Hot Southern Honey (mild or hot), for drizzling

Kosher salt, to taste

Freshly ground black pepper, to taste

8 fresh chive stalks

1. For the eggs, fill a large skillet two-thirds full of water and add the vinegar. Place over medium-high heat.

2. Adjust the oven rack 6 inches (15 cm) from the top. Preheat the broiler to high.

3. For the ham, heat a large skillet (preferably cast iron) over medium heat and let it get nice and hot.

4. Cut the ham steaks into eight pieces that will fit on the English muffin halves. Add them to the skillet and cook for 1 to 2 minutes per side, until seared. Drizzle the tops with hot honey, flip, sear, and repeat a couple of times until the ham is lacquered with honey.

5. Once the water for the eggs is at a bare simmer, crack each egg, one at a time, into a small ramekin and gently slide the egg into the water. Let them poach for 3 to 4 minutes, until the whites are set but the yolks are soft. Using a slotted spoon, lift them onto a paper towel–lined plate.

6. Split the English muffins and place, cut sides down, on a rimmed sheet pan. Broil for 1 to 2 minutes per side, until toasted, then butter them.

7. Divide the English muffin halves among plates and top each one with a piece of ham and a poached egg.

8. Sprinkle the eggs with salt and pepper, then use kitchen scissors to snip the chives into small pieces over the tops. Serve immediately.

Goat Cheese and Tomato Omelet

5 minutes · *Serves 1*

2 large eggs

⅛ teaspoon kosher salt

⅛ teaspoon freshly ground black pepper, plus more for serving

1 teaspoon unsalted butter

6 grape or cherry tomatoes, quartered

¼ cup (60 g) fresh goat cheese

AR's Hot Southern Honey (mild or hot), for drizzling

3 fresh chive stalks, for serving

1. In a small bowl, beat together the eggs, salt, and pepper with a fork.
2. Place a medium nonstick skillet over medium heat. Once it's hot, add the butter and swirl to coat the bottom of the skillet.
3. Pour in the beaten eggs (they will cover the bottom of the skillet). Let cook, without stirring, for about 1 minute, or until the eggs are almost set.
4. Scatter the tomatoes and crumble the cheese over the eggs.
5. Using a silicone spatula, fold the eggs over themselves into a little package. Slide the omelet onto a plate and drizzle with some hot honey.
6. Use kitchen scissors to snip the chives into small pieces over the top, then sprinkle with a little more pepper. Serve immediately.

Savory Dutch Baby with Prosciutto and Parmesan

25 minutes   *Serves 4*

3 large eggs

½ cup (60 g) all-purpose flour

¾ cup (175 ml) whole milk

¼ cup (65 g) grated Parmesan, plus more for serving

8 fresh chive stalks, chopped, plus more for serving

1 teaspoon fresh thyme leaves

½ teaspoon kosher salt

2 tablespoons unsalted butter

4 very thin slices prosciutto

AR's Hot Southern Honey (mild or hot), for drizzling

1. Preheat the oven to 425°F (220°C; gas mark 7). Place a 10-inch (25 cm) cast-iron skillet in the oven while it preheats to get the skillet nice and hot.

2. In a medium bowl, whisk together the eggs. Add the flour and whisk until smooth, then gradually whisk in the milk. Whisk in the Parmesan, chopped chives, thyme, and salt.

3. Take the skillet out of the oven and add the butter (it will melt quickly). Once it melts, pour in the batter, then slide the skillet back into the oven.

4. Bake for about 20 minutes, or until golden brown and puffed.

5. Top the Dutch baby with the prosciutto, a little more Parmesan and chopped chives, and a generous drizzle of hot honey. Slice and serve immediately.

Bourbon Pecan Coffee Cake

 1 hour 5 minutes ❖ *Serves 8*

Topping

1 cup (100 g) pecans, chopped

3 tablespoons dark brown sugar

2 tablespoons AR's Hot Southern Honey (mild)

¼ teaspoon ground cinnamon

¼ teaspoon kosher salt

2 tablespoons unsalted butter, melted

Cake

Nonstick vegetable oil cooking spray, for the pan

1¾ cups (210 g) all-purpose flour

¾ teaspoon baking powder

¾ teaspoon baking soda

½ teaspoon kosher salt

½ cup (1 stick, or 115 g) unsalted butter, at room temperature

¾ cup (150 g) granulated sugar

2 large eggs

1 tablespoon bourbon whiskey

¾ cup (170 g) sour cream

1. Preheat the oven to 350°F (175°C). Spray a 4½ × 8½-inch (11 × 21 cm) loaf pan with cooking spray. Line the bottom of the pan with parchment paper, leaving an overhang on the two long sides (for easy lifting once the cake is baked). Set aside.

2. To make the topping: In a small bowl, stir together the pecans, brown sugar, hot honey, cinnamon, ¼ teaspoon salt, and butter. Set aside.

3. To make the cake: In a medium bowl, whisk together the flour, baking powder, baking soda, and ½ teaspoon salt.

4. In a large bowl using an electric mixer or in the bowl of a stand mixer, beat together the butter and sugar on medium-high speed for 1 to 2 minutes, until fluffy. Beat in the eggs until creamy, then beat in the bourbon.

5. Add half of the dry ingredients to the wet ingredients and mix on low speed. Mix in the sour cream, then mix in the remaining dry ingredients.

6. Evenly spread half of the batter into the prepared pan. Crumble in half of the topping over the batter. Scrape the remaining batter into the pan and spread evenly. Crumble the remaining topping over the batter.

7. Bake for 48 to 50 minutes, until a toothpick inserted in the center comes out with a few moist crumbs attached. Let cool for 10 minutes on a wire cooling rack. Grab the edges of the parchment and lift out. Let cool completely before slicing.

Yogurt with Almond Clusters and Blueberry Compote

45 minutes *Serves 8*

Almond Clusters

1 cup (80 g) old-fashioned rolled oats

1 cup (90 g) sliced almonds

½ cup (35 g) unsweetened shredded coconut

¼ cup (85 g) AR's Hot Southern Honey (mild), plus more for drizzling

2 tablespoons dark brown sugar

1 tablespoon coconut oil

1 teaspoon pure vanilla extract

¾ teaspoon kosher salt

¼ teaspoon ground cinnamon

Blueberry Compote

1 (10-ounce, or 280-g) package frozen or fresh blueberries (about 2¼ cups)

3 tablespoons AR's Hot Southern Honey (mild)

3 tablespoons fresh orange juice

Small pinch kosher salt

Serving

16 ounces (454 g) Greek or regular plain yogurt

1. Preheat the oven to 300°F (150°C; gas mark 2). Line a large rimmed sheet pan with parchment paper and set aside.

2. To make the almond clusters: In a large bowl, combine the oats, almonds, and coconut.

3. Whisk together the ¼ cup (85 g) hot honey, brown sugar, coconut oil, vanilla, ¾ teaspoon salt, and cinnamon in a small skillet over medium heat for 1 to 2 minutes, until melted. Pour over the oat mixture and stir well to combine.

4. Pour the almond cluster mixture onto the prepared pan and spread into a thin layer.

5. Bake for 35 to 40 minutes, until dark golden brown. Gently stir halfway through baking time, taking care not to break up the clusters. Let cool completely (it will crisp up as it cools).

6. To make the blueberry compote: In a small saucepan, combine the blueberries, 3 tablespoons hot honey, orange juice, and pinch of salt over medium-high heat. Simmer for 5 to 8 minutes, until the blueberries start to break down and the juices start to thicken. Let cool.

7. To serve: For each bowl, spoon in some yogurt and compote. Top with almond clusters and drizzle with a little more hot honey.

Toast with Fresh Ricotta and Strawberries

5 minutes ❈ *Serves 2*

2 slices of your favorite bread to toast

½ cup (125 g) fresh ricotta

6 strawberries, sliced

AR's Hot Southern Honey (mild or hot), for drizzling

1 tablespoon chopped pistachios or hemp hearts

1 orange, for zesting

Fresh chopped mint leaves (optional)

1. Toast the bread and top with the ricotta and sliced strawberries.

2. Drizzle with hot honey.

3. Sprinkle with the pistachios or hemp hearts, grate some orange zest over the tops, and sprinkle with mint (if using).

appetizers

Spicy Korean-Style Chicken Wings

25 minutes *Serves 4 to 6*

2 pounds (907 g) chicken wings

¾ teaspoon kosher salt

¼ teaspoon freshly ground
black pepper

⅓ cup (90 g) gochujang (Korean
red chile paste)

2 tablespoons less-sodium soy sauce

2 tablespoons AR's Hot Southern Honey
(mild or hot)

2 teaspoons unseasoned rice vinegar

2 teaspoons toasted sesame oil

2 cloves garlic, grated

2 scallions, thinly sliced, for serving

1. Preheat the grill to medium-high.

2. Season the wings with the salt and pepper.

3. In a large bowl, stir together the gochujang, soy sauce, hot honey,
   vinegar, sesame oil, and garlic.

4. Grill the wings for 4 to 5 minutes per side, until the skin is golden
   brown and crisp.

5. Add the wings to the large bowl with the sauce and toss well to coat.

6. Return the wings to the grill, turning and basting with the remaining sauce,
   until the wings are lacquered and charred.

7. Top with the sliced scallions. Serve immediately.

Corn Fritters with Avocado and Hot Honey

30 minutes *Makes 16 fritters*

1 medium yellow onion, quartered

¾ cup (45 g) fresh cilantro

1 large egg

3 cups (435 g) fresh or frozen (thawed) corn

1 tablespoon AR's Hot Southern Honey (mild or hot), plus more for drizzling

¾ cup (90 g) all-purpose flour

¼ cup (35 g) finely ground cornmeal

1 teaspoon baking powder

1½ teaspoons kosher salt, plus more for serving

1½ teaspoons ground cumin

1 teaspoon ground coriander

¼ teaspoon freshly ground black pepper

Extra-virgin olive oil, for frying

1 avocado, sliced, for serving

4 scallions (white and light green parts), chopped, for serving

1. In a food processor, pulse the onion pieces and cilantro three or four times until chopped. Add the egg and corn and pulse a few times until blended but not smooth, leaving some corn kernels intact. Pour into a medium bowl.

2. Stir in the hot honey. Add the flour, cornmeal, baking powder, salt, cumin, coriander, and pepper. Stir to combine.

3. Heat about ⅛ inch (3 mm) of oil in a large skillet over medium-high heat. Line a plate with two paper towels and set aside.

4. To test if the oil is hot, add a drop of batter to the oil. It should sizzle immediately. Cooking in batches to avoid overcrowding, spoon in about 2 tablespoons of batter for each fritter, flattening them slightly and spacing them about 1 inch (2.5 cm) apart. Cook for 1½ to 2 minutes per side, until golden brown and cooked through. Transfer to the prepared plate. Add more oil to the skillet as necessary.

5. Top the fritters with slices of avocado and a little salt. Sprinkle with the chopped scallions and drizzle with hot honey. Serve immediately.

Crispy Cornmeal Fries with Parmesan and Mint

1 hour 20 minutes *Serves 4 to 6*

Nonstick vegetable oil cooking spray, for the pan

3 cups (700 ml) water

1 cup (140 g) finely ground cornmeal

1 wedge Parmesan

10 fresh mint leaves, chopped

1¼ teaspoons kosher salt

Extra-virgin olive oil, for frying

AR's Hot Southern Honey (mild or hot), for drizzling

1. Spray an 8 × 8-inch (20 × 20 cm) square baking pan with cooking spray. Set aside.

2. In a medium saucepan, bring the water to a boil over medium-high heat. Add the cornmeal while whisking constantly to avoid lumps. Continue to whisk as the mixture comes together. Reduce the heat to medium-low and cook for 12 to 15 minutes, whisking often, until the cornmeal is tender and has thickened and pulls away from the sides of the pan. Remove from the heat.

3. Grate ⅓ cup (33 g) of cheese from the Parmesan wedge. Whisk in the grated cheese along with the mint and salt.

4. Scrape the mixture into the prepared pan and spread evenly. Refrigerate for at least 1 hour or overnight.

5. Turn out the cornmeal square onto a cutting board. Slice into 4-inch-long (10 cm) by ¾-inch-wide (2 cm) fries.

6. Heat ¼ inch (6 mm) of oil in a large skillet (preferably cast iron) over medium-high heat. Line a plate with two paper towels and set aside.

7. To test if the oil is hot, add a little piece of cornmeal mixture to the pan. It should cook immediately. Cooking in batches to avoid overcrowding and adding more oil as necessary, add the fries and cook for 8 to 10 minutes, turning them occasionally, until golden brown and crisp. Transfer to the prepared plate.

8. Arrange the fries on a serving plate. Using a vegetable peeler, peel wide strips of Parmesan from the wedge over the fries.

9. Drizzle with hot honey and serve immediately.

Whipped Feta Dip

5 minutes *Serves 4 to 6*

8 ounces (227 g) feta cheese, crumbled (2 cups)

½ cup (115 g) Greek yogurt

1 tablespoon AR's Hot Southern Honey (mild or hot), plus more for drizzling

Fresh thyme leaves, for serving

Chopped chives, for serving

Crunchy vegetables, for serving

Grilled bread, for serving

1. In a food processor, combine the feta, yogurt, and honey. Blend until smooth and creamy.

2. Spoon the whipped feta into a serving bowl and top with the thyme and chives.

3. Drizzle with honey.

4. Serve with crunchy vegetables and grilled bread.

Kumquat Chutney with Goat Cheese and Crackers

25 minutes *Serves 6 to 8*

12 kumquats, thinly sliced into rounds

1 small red onion, very thinly sliced

½ jalapeño pepper, seeded, if desired, and very thinly sliced

½ cup (170 g) AR's Hot Southern Honey (mild or hot)

¼ cup (60 ml) white wine vinegar

¼ teaspoon kosher salt, plus more to taste

1 (8-ounce, or 227-g) log goat cheese, for serving

Crackers, for serving

1. In a small saucepan, combine the kumquats, onion, jalapeño, hot honey, vinegar, and salt over medium-high heat. Let the mixture come to a boil, then reduce to a simmer. Simmer for about 20 minutes, or until the chutney starts to thicken, stirring occasionally.

2. Let cool to room temperature, then refrigerate to cool completely. When ready to serve, taste for salt; you may want to add a little more.

3. Serve with the goat cheese and crackers.

Popovers with Hot Honey and Flaky Sea Salt

35 minutes *Makes 12 popovers*

2 tablespoons unsalted butter, melted, plus more for pan

3 large eggs, at room temperature

1¼ cups (300 ml) whole milk

1 cup (120 g) all-purpose flour

½ teaspoon kosher salt

AR's Hot Southern Honey (mild or hot), for drizzling

Flaky sea salt, for serving

1. Preheat the oven to 425°F (220°C; gas mark 7). Generously butter a 12-cup muffin pan (or two 6-cup muffin pans) and set aside.

2. In a large bowl, whisk together the eggs, then whisk in about half of the milk. Add the flour and kosher salt and whisk until smooth. Whisk in the remaining milk and the melted butter.

3. Pour the batter into a large liquid measuring cup for easy pouring.

4. Place the muffin pan in the oven for 3 minutes to warm it.

5. Dividing evenly, pour the batter into the prepared muffin cups, filling each cup about halfway.

6. Bake for 22 to 25 minutes, until golden brown and puffed (do not open the oven beforehand or they will deflate).

7. Drizzle with hot honey and sprinkled with a little flaky sea salt. Serve immediately.

Fried Squash Blossoms with Hot Honey and Oregano

15 minutes ❈ Serves 4

8 zucchini squash blossoms

Extra-virgin olive oil, for frying

½ cup (60 g) all-purpose flour

2 tablespoons cornstarch

⅛ teaspoon baking soda

½ cup (60 ml) ice-cold sparkling water

AR's Hot Southern Honey (mild or hot), for drizzling

Flaky sea salt, for serving

Fresh oregano leaves, torn, for serving

1. Carefully remove the pistil from the inside of each of the squash blossoms while leaving the flowers intact.

2. In a medium saucepan, heat 1 inch (2.5 cm) of oil over medium-high heat. Line a plate with two paper towels and set aside.

3. In a small bowl, whisk together the flour, cornstarch, and baking soda. While whisking, slowly pour in the sparkling water until the mixture is smooth. It should resemble thin pancake batter.

4. To test if the oil is hot, add a drop of batter to the oil. It should sizzle immediately. Holding the stem, dip a squash blossom into the batter, turning to coat completely, then add to the oil. Repeat with a few more blossoms, without overcrowding the pan. Fry for about 1 minute, turning them halfway through, until light golden brown and crisp. Transfer to the prepared plate. Repeat with the remaining squash blossoms and batter.

5. Drizzle the blossoms with hot honey and sprinkle with a little salt and oregano. Serve immediately.

Watermelon Wedges with Cucumber-Feta Salsa

15 minutes *Serves 4*

1 cucumber, peeled and cut into ¼-inch (6 mm) dice

¼ medium red onion, chopped

½ jalapeño pepper, seeded, if desired, and chopped

2 tablespoons extra-virgin olive oil

1 tablespoon fresh lemon juice

⅛ teaspoon kosher salt

¼ teaspoon freshly ground black pepper

2 ounces (56 g) feta cheese, crumbled (½ cup)

8 leaves fresh basil, torn

12 to 16 wedges watermelon, cut ½ inch (1 cm) thick

AR's Hot Southern Honey (mild or hot), for drizzling

1. In a small bowl, stir together the cucumber, onion, jalapeño, oil, lemon juice, salt, and pepper.

2. Fold in the feta and basil.

3. For serving, arrange the watermelon wedges on a platter and spoon on the cucumber-feta salsa.

4. Drizzle with hot honey.

Quick Pickled Green Beans

15 minutes, plus 24 hours pickling time *Serves 4*

2½ cups (10 ounces, or 280 g)
 fresh green beans, trimmed

3 sprigs fresh dill

1¼ cups (300 ml) white wine vinegar

1¼ cups (300 ml) water

¼ cup (85 g) AR's Hot Southern
Honey (mild or hot)

½ teaspoon black peppercorns

½ teaspoon whole coriander seeds

1 teaspoon kosher salt

1. Tightly pack the green beans and dill in a 1-quart (950 ml) glass jar, leaving ½ inch (1 cm) of space at the top.

2. In a small saucepan, combine the vinegar, water, hot honey, peppercorns, coriander seeds, and salt. Place over medium-high heat and let come to a boil. Pour into the jar of green beans.

3. Let cool to room temperature, seal with a lid, and refrigerate for at least 24 hours and up to 2 weeks.

Ricotta and Peach Crostini with Hot Honey

CONTRIBUTED BY HELEN RUSSELL

30 minutes · *Serves 4 to 6*

2 cups (250 g) fresh ricotta

2 pinches of salt

2 cracks of freshly ground black pepper

2 tablespoons AR's Hot Southern Honey (mild or hot), plus more for drizzling

½ cup (65 g) roasted pistachios, shelled

1 standard baguette, sliced into ½-inch-thick (1 cm) slices

1 tablespoon butter, melted

1 peach

¼ cup (10 g) chopped fresh basil

1. Preheat the oven to 350°F (175°C; gas mark 4). Line two baking sheets with parchment paper and set aside.
2. In a large bowl or food processor, combine the ricotta, salt, pepper, and 2 tablespoons hot honey. Whisk or blend until smooth. Set aside.
3. Lightly crush the pistachios. The quickest and easiest way to do this is to add them to a resealable plastic bag and, using a roller or nonstick cooking spray bottle, crush them.
4. Transfer the pistachios to one of the prepared baking sheets and toast in the oven for 5 minutes, or until lightly browned.
5. Place the baguette slices in a single layer on the other prepared baking sheet. Brush the tops of the slices with the melted butter, then toast in the oven for about 5 minutes, or until golden.
6. Meanwhile, slice the peach into 1/4-inch-thick (6 mm) slices.
7. Top each crostino with some of the ricotta mixture and two or three pear slices. Sprinkle with the chopped basil and toasted pistachios and finish with a drizzle of hot honey.

Spicy Candied Pecans

10 minutes ❈ *Serves 6 to 8*

2 cups (200 g) raw pecans

¼ cup (85 g) AR's Hot Southern Honey (mild or hot)

¼ cup (50 g) sugar

¼ cup (60 ml) water

Kosher salt, for sprinkling

1. Line a rimmed sheet pan with parchment paper. Set aside.

2. Stir together the pecans, hot honey, sugar, and water in a medium skillet over medium-high heat. Once the honey mixture comes to a boil, stir constantly for about 5 minutes, or until all the water has evaporated and the mixture thickens. Continue to stir for another 1 to 2 minutes, until the mixture turns a deep golden brown and caramelizes around the pecans.

3. Quickly spread out the pecans on the prepared pan. Be careful not to touch them; they are extremely hot! Sprinkle with a little salt.

4. Let the pecans cool completely (they will crisp up as they cool).

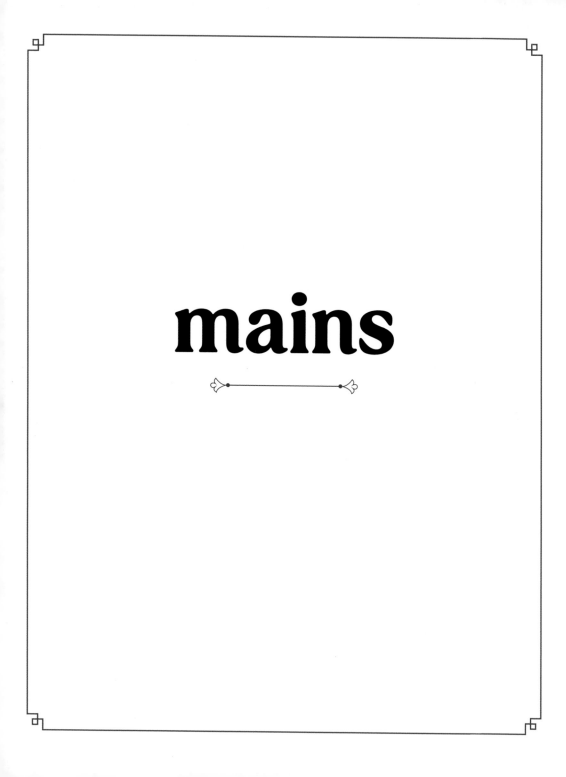

mains

Smoky Barbecue Ribs

3 hours 15 minutes *Serves 4 to 6*

Barbecue Rub

¼ cup (28 g) smoked paprika

2 tablespoons onion powder

2 tablespoons garlic powder

2 tablespoons dark brown sugar

4 teaspoons freshly ground
black pepper

2 teaspoons kosher salt

Ribs

4 pounds (1.8 kg) pork spareribs

2 teaspoons kosher salt

Barbecue Sauce

1 cup (240 g) ketchup

⅔ cup (155 ml) apple cider vinegar

¼ cup (85 g) AR's Hot Southern Honey (mild or hot)

¼ cup (28 g) Barbecue Rub

1. To make the barbecue rub: In a small bowl, combine the smoked paprika, onion powder, garlic powder, brown sugar, pepper, and 2 teaspoons salt.

2. To make the ribs: Preheat the oven to 300°F (150°C; gas mark 2).

3. Cut the ribs in half so you have two manageable pieces to work with. Sprinkle them with the 2 teaspoons salt. Reserve ¼ cup (28 g) of the barbecue rub for the barbecue sauce, then sprinkle the remaining rub over the ribs. Wrap each portion tightly in foil and place on a large rimmed sheet pan.

4. Bake for 3 hours, or until the meat is fork tender but not falling off the bone. Open the foil to let out the steam. (The ribs can be baked a day or two ahead; just let cool to room temperature, close up the foil, and refrigerate.)

5. While the ribs bake, make the barbecue sauce: In a small bowl, stir together the ketchup, vinegar, hot honey, and the reserved barbecue rub.

6. Preheat the grill to medium-high.

7. Place the ribs directly on the grill and grill for about 10 minutes, turning and basting them often with the barbecue sauce, until they are lacquered and charred.

8. Cut between the ribs to separate into single ribs. Serve the ribs with any extra barbecue sauce.

Panfried Hot Honey Chicken Sandwiches with Pickle Mayonnaise

35 minutes, plus 1 hour brining time *Serves 4*

Chicken

1 cup (240 ml) water

3 teaspoons kosher salt, divided

2 tablespoons AR's Hot Southern Honey (mild or hot), plus more for drizzling

4 (4-ounce, or 115-g) boneless, skinless chicken thighs

1 cup (120 g) all-purpose flour

2 teaspoons onion powder

½ teaspoon freshly ground black pepper

½ teaspoon cayenne pepper

½ cup (120 ml) buttermilk

Canola or grapeseed oil, for frying

4 potato buns

2 tablespoons unsalted butter

8 butter lettuce leaves

Pickle Mayonnaise

½ cup (115 g) mayonnaise

½ cup (68 g) chopped dill pickles

¼ cup (40 g) chopped sweet or red onion

2 teaspoons fresh lemon juice

½ teaspoon Worcestershire sauce

¼ teaspoon kosher salt

⅛ teaspoon freshly ground black pepper

1. To make the chicken: In a small saucepan, combine the water, 2 teaspoons of the salt, and the hot honey. Place over medium-high heat and let come to a boil. Pour the brine into a heatproof, nonreactive bowl and let cool. Refrigerate, uncovered, until completely cold.

2. Add the chicken thighs to the brine (it should be submerged), cover, and refrigerate for at least 1 hour and up to 24 hours (the longer the better).

3. To make the pickle mayonnaise: In a small bowl, stir together the mayonnaise, pickles, onion, lemon juice, Worcestershire sauce, ¼ teaspoon salt, and ⅛ teaspoon black pepper. Refrigerate while you fry the chicken.

(continued on page 60)

(continued from page 58)

4. When ready to fry the chicken, set up your breading station. In a medium bowl, whisk together the flour, onion powder, ½ teaspoon black pepper, cayenne pepper, and remaining 1 teaspoon salt. Pour the buttermilk into another medium bowl.

5. Heat ½ inch (1 cm) of oil in a high-sided skillet (preferably cast iron) over medium-high heat to between to 325° and 350°F (170° and 180°C). Line a plate with two paper towels and set aside.

6. Remove the chicken thighs from the brine, rinse, and pat dry. Add the chicken thighs to the buttermilk, turning to coat. Working with one thigh at a time, lift the chicken out of the buttermilk, letting the excess drip off. Dredge the chicken in the flour mixture, patting the mixture over the surface and into the crevices to make sure it is well coated.

7. Carefully lower the chicken thighs into the oil and fry for 4 to 5 minutes per side, turning as you go, until the crust is deep golden brown and crisp and the chicken is cooked through. Transfer to the prepared plate.

8. To heat the buns, melt 1 tablespoon of the butter in a medium skillet over medium heat. Add two of the buns, cut sides down, and cook until the undersides are toasted. Repeat with the remaining butter and buns.

9. Build the sandwiches in the following order (or however you like): the bottom bun, one chicken thigh, a drizzle of hot honey, some pickle mayonnaise, two lettuce leaves, and the top bun. Serve immediately.

Grilled Pork Chops with Peaches and Scallions

1 hour 35 minutes Serves 4

6 cloves garlic, very finely chopped

2 tablespoons chopped fresh rosemary

1 tablespoon chopped fresh thyme leaves

3 tablespoons extra-virgin olive oil, plus more for the peaches and scallions

4 (12-ounce, or 340-g) bone-in pork loin chops, about 1 inch (2.5 cm) thick

1¼ teaspoons plus ⅛ teaspoon kosher salt, divided

¼ teaspoon plus ⅛ teaspoon freshly ground black pepper, divided

12 scallions, trimmed

4 peaches, halved, pits removed

AR's Hot Southern Honey (mild or hot), for grilling and serving

1. In a small bowl, combine the garlic, rosemary, thyme, and 3 tablespoons oil.

2. Season both sides of the pork chops with 1¼ teaspoons of the salt and ¼ teaspoon of the pepper. Put them in a baking dish and rub both sides with the garlic marinade. Cover and let marinate for at least 1 hour in the refrigerator or overnight.

3. Before you grill, let the pork chops come to room temperature (about 20 minutes). Preheat the grill to medium-high.

4. Grill the pork chops for 5 to 6 minutes per side (for medium), until nicely charred. Let rest for 5 minutes before serving.

5. Meanwhile, toss the scallions and peaches in a little oil, just to coat. Sprinkle with the remaining ⅛ teaspoon each of salt and pepper.

6. Grill the scallions for 3 to 4 minutes, until charred. Grill the peaches for 1 to 2 minutes per side, until grill marks form. Drizzle hot honey on the cut sides of the peaches. Turn them over and grill so the honey sears into the peaches. Repeat drizzling with honey and searing two more times, until there is a nice layer of charred honey on the peaches..

7. Serve the pork with the scallions, peaches, and a drizzle of hot honey.

Hot Honey Spoon Bread

CONTRIBUTED BY WALTER BUNDY

30 minutes *Serves 6*

Spoon Bread

¼ cup (½ stick, or 60 g) unsalted butter, plus more for buttering the ramekins

½ gallon (64 ounces, or 1.9 L) whole milk

⅓ cup (65 g) sugar

2 cups (280 g) yellow cornmeal

3 large eggs

½ cup (60 g) all-purpose flour

1½ teaspoons baking powder

Salt, to taste

Freshly ground white pepper, to taste

Garnish

2 tablespoons unsalted butter

1 pound (454 g) fresh jumbo lump crabmeat

½ pound (227 g) salt- or sugar-cured Virginia country ham, shaved thinly (such as Kite's Country Hams brand)

AR's Hot Southern Honey (mild or hot), for drizzling

5 or 6 fresh chive stalks, chopped, for serving

1. Preheat the oven to 345°F (175°C; gas mark 3). Butter six 10-ounce (300 ml) ramekins and set aside.

2. To make the spoon bread: In a large saucepan, bring the milk, sugar, and ¼ cup (60 g) butter to a boil over medium-high heat.

3. Whisk in the cornmeal and cook until it is slightly thickened, about 5 minutes. Remove from the heat and let cool slightly. Whisk in the eggs, flour, and baking powder until incorporated evenly. Season with salt and pepper.

4. Dividing evenly, ladle the spoon bread batter into the prepared ramekins and place the ramekins in a water bath.

5. Bake for 18 to 20 minutes, until the tops are golden brown. Let cool for 5 minutes.

6. When the spoon bread is almost done baking at 15 minutes, make the garnish: In a large skillet, melt the 2 tablespoons butter over medium-high heat until golden.

7. Add the crabmeat and country ham to the pan, gently fold, and warm.

8. Once warm, scoop the crabmeat and ham onto the spoon bread in the ramekins.

9. Drizzle hot honey over the crabmeat, ham, and spoon bread. Sprinkle the chopped chives on top and serve.

Chicken and Cabbage Salad with Ginger Dressing and Crispy Wontons

30 minutes *Serves 4*

Salad

3 (6- to 8-ounce, or 170- to 228-g) boneless, skinless chicken breasts

8 cups (560 g) shredded napa cabbage

1 cup (130 g) grated carrots (about 2 medium carrots)

8 radishes, thinly sliced

3 scallions (white and light green parts), thinly sliced

½ cup (30 g) fresh cilantro leaves

¼ cup (15 g) fresh mint leaves, torn

Dressing

3 tablespoons fresh orange juice

3 tablespoons extra-virgin olive oil

2 tablespoons fresh lime juice

1 tablespoon AR's Hot Southern Honey (mild or hot)

1 teaspoon toasted sesame oil

1 tablespoon grated ginger

¾ teaspoon kosher salt

¼ teaspoon freshly ground black pepper

Crispy Wonton Strips

16 wonton skins

Extra-virgin olive oil, for frying

AR's Hot Southern Honey (mild or hot), for drizzling

Kosher salt, to taste

1. To make the salad: Put the chicken breast in a medium saucepan and cover with cold water by 2 inches (5 cm) to poach them. Place over medium-high heat and let come to a boil. Once the water starts to boil, remove the pan from the heat, cover tightly with a lid, and let stand for 15 minutes. Take the chicken out of the water and let cool.

2. To make the dressing: In a small bowl, whisk together the orange juice, olive oil, lime juice, hot honey, sesame oil, ginger, salt, and pepper.

(continued on page 66)

(continued from page 64)

3. Shred the cooled chicken and put it in a medium bowl. Drizzle with 3 tablespoons of the dressing and toss. Let marinate while you assemble the salad.

4. In a large bowl, combine the cabbage, carrots, radishes, scallions, cilantro, and mint. Add the remaining dressing and toss. Add the marinated chicken and toss once more.

5. To make the crispy wontons: Cut the wonton skins into ½-inch-wide (1 cm) strips. Toss them to separate.

6. Heat ⅛ inch (3 mm) of oil in a medium skillet over medium-high heat. Line a plate with two paper towels and set aside.

7. To test if the oil is hot, add a wonton strip to the oil. It should cook immediately. Add half of the wonton strips to the skillet and cook for 2 to 3 minutes, stirring, until golden brown. Transfer to the prepared plate. Repeat with the remaining wonton strips.

8. Drizzle the crispy strips with a little hot honey and sprinkle with salt.

9. Divide the salad among bowls and top with the crispy wonton strips.

Hot Honey Rosemary Chicken under a Brick

 1 hour 20 minutes   *Serves 4*

8 bone-in, skin-on chicken thighs (2½ to 3 pounds, or 1.1 to 1.4 kg)

1 teaspoon kosher salt

½ teaspoon freshly ground black pepper

3 tablespoons extra-virgin olive oil, divided

2 cloves garlic, finely chopped

2 teaspoons chopped fresh rosemary

½ teaspoon paprika

AR's Hot Southern Honey (mild or hot), for drizzling

1. Season both sides of the chicken with the salt and pepper.

2. In a large bowl, combine 2 tablespoons of the oil, the garlic, rosemary, and paprika. Add the chicken to the bowl and toss to coat. Cover and let marinate in the refrigerator for at least 1 hour or overnight.

3. Heat the remaining 1 tablespoon oil in a large skillet (preferably cast iron) over medium-high heat.

4. Place the chicken, skin side down, in the skillet. Lay a piece of parchment paper over the chicken. Place another skillet on top of the chicken and weigh it down with another heavy pan, a large can of tomatoes, or a brick.

5. Cook for about 12 minutes, or until the skin is deep golden brown and crisp. Flip the chicken and weigh it down again. Continue to cook for 5 to 8 minutes more, until cooked through. Remove the top skillet and weight.

6. Drizzle with hot honey and serve.

Lettuce Cups with Grilled Hot Honey and Soy Sauce–Marinated Steak

45 minutes *Serves 4*

Steak

¼ cup (60 ml) less-sodium soy sauce

1 tablespoon AR's Hot Southern Honey (mild or hot)

2 cloves garlic, grated

1½ pounds (680 g) skirt steak, flank steak, or sirloin flap, very thinly sliced against the grain

Pinch of kosher salt

Dressing

¼ cup (60 ml) unseasoned rice vinegar

2 tablespoons AR's Hot Southern Honey (mild or hot)

¼ teaspoon kosher salt

Lettuce Cups

12 to 16 large butter lettuce leaves

1 cucumber, thinly sliced

1 red bell pepper, thinly sliced

3 cups (495 g) cooked white rice

4 scallions (white and light green parts), thinly sliced

1. To make the steak: In a large bowl, whisk together the soy sauce, 1 tablespoon hot honey, and garlic. Add the steak slices, cover, and let marinate in the refrigerator for at least 30 minutes or overnight.

2. To make the dressing: In a small bowl, whisk together the vinegar, 2 tablespoons hot honey, and ¼ teaspoon salt. Set aside.

3. Preheat the grill to medium-high. Take the steak slices out of the marinade and lay on a plate. Sprinkle with the pinch of salt. Grill for 4 to 5 minutes, turning occasionally, until charred and cooked through.

4. To serve, place the components on small plates or a platter to allow each person to assemble their own lettuce cups.

5. To assemble the lettuce cups, fill each lettuce leaf with some cucumber slices, bell pepper strips, and rice. Drizzle with the dressing and top with the steak and scallion slices. Fold and eat.

Grilled Steak with Roasted Garlic and Blue Cheese Butter

1 hour ❖ *Serves 4 to 6*

Butter

2 small heads garlic

2 teaspoons extra-virgin olive oil

¼ teaspoon kosher salt, plus a pinch for the garlic

⅛ teaspoon freshly ground black pepper, plus a pinch for the garlic

½ cup (1 stick, or 115 g) unsalted butter, at room temperature

⅓ cup (40 g) blue cheese, at room temperature

2 tablespoons AR's Hot Southern Honey (mild or hot)

2 teaspoons fresh thyme leaves

Steaks

4 (10- to 12-ounce, or 280- to 340-g) strip steaks, about 1 inch (2.5 cm) thick

1½ teaspoons kosher salt

½ teaspoon freshly ground black pepper

1. Preheat the oven to 400°F (205°C; gas mark 6).

2. To make the butter: Trim off the tops of the garlic heads to expose the cloves. Place the garlic heads on a large piece of foil, drizzle them with the olive oil, and sprinkle with a pinch each of the salt and pepper. Wrap tightly and roast for about 40 minutes, or until the cloves are tender. Let cool.

3. In a small bowl, mash together the butter, blue cheese, hot honey, thyme, and the remaining ¼ teaspoon salt and ⅛ teaspoon pepper. Squeeze the roasted garlic cloves into the butter and mash them in. Serve the butter in a bowl, or place it on a piece of parchment paper, shape into a log, roll up, and refrigerate until set, then slice for serving.

4. To make the steaks: Let the steaks come to room temperature (about 20 minutes). Preheat the grill to medium-high.

5. Once at room temperature, season the steaks with the 1½ teaspoons salt and ½ teaspoon pepper.

6. Grill the steaks for 4 to 6 minutes on the first side, until a nice crust forms. Flip the steaks and grill for 4 to 6 minutes more for medium-rare, until an instant-read thermometer reads 125°F (51°C) when inserted in the middle of the steak (or cook until desired doneness). Let the steaks rest for 5 minutes.

7. Serve topped with a spoonful or slice of the butter.

Black-Eyed Peas and Rice–Stuffed Peppers

2 hours   ❋   *Serves 4*

¾ cup (188 g) dried black-eyed peas, rinsed

1¾ teaspoons kosher salt, divided

3 ounces (85 g) bacon, cut crosswise into ½-inch (1 cm) pieces

1 medium yellow onion, chopped

2 ribs celery, chopped

1 clove garlic, finely chopped

1 tablespoon tomato paste

2 tablespoons apple cider vinegar

2 tablespoons AR's Hot Southern Honey (mild or hot)

¼ teaspoon freshly ground black pepper

¾ cup (138 g) long-grain white rice

1½ cups (350 ml) water

2 tablespoons chopped fresh flat-leaf parsley

4 red bell peppers

Extra-virgin olive oil, for drizzling

1. To cook the black-eyed peas (no need to soak), combine the black-eyed peas and 1 teaspoon of the salt in a medium saucepan. Add cold water to cover by 2 inches (5 cm) and place over medium-high heat. Let come to a boil. Cover partially with a lid and reduce the heat so that the beans simmer gently. Cook for 45 to 60 minutes, until tender (the older the beans the longer the cooking time). Drain.

2. While the black-eyed peas cook, cook the bacon in a large pot over medium-high heat for 6 to 7 minutes, until crisp. Add the onion and celery and cook, stirring occasionally, for 12 to 15 minutes, until the onion and celery are very tender.

3. Stir in the garlic and cook for 1 minute. Add the tomato paste and cook, stirring, for 1 minute. Stir in the vinegar, hot honey, and black pepper. Add the rice and cook, stirring, for 1 minute. Stir in the black-eyed peas, water, and the remaining ¾ teaspoon salt and let come to a boil. Cover tightly with a lid, reduce the heat to low, and cook for 20 to 25 minutes, until the rice is tender. Stir in the parsley.

4. Preheat the oven to 375°F (190°C; gas mark 5).

5. While the rice cooks, cut out the tops from the bell peppers at the "shoulders" to make lids. Cut out the white membranes from the insides of the peppers and shake out the seeds. Trim the white membranes from the lids too.

6. Dividing evenly, fill the peppers with the rice mixture and top with the lids. Place them in a baking dish and add enough water to cover the bottom of the dish by ¼ inch (6 mm). Drizzle the peppers with a little oil.

7. Bake for about 1 hour, or until the peppers are tender. Serve hot.

Shrimp and Grits

40 minutes *Serves 4*

Grits

4 cups (950 ml) water

1 cup (135 g) yellow or white grits (not instant)

2 tablespoons unsalted butter

1 tablespoon AR's Hot Southern Honey (mild or hot)

1 teaspoon kosher salt

Shrimp

1 tablespoon unsalted butter

1 clove garlic, finely chopped

2 large, ripe beefsteak tomatoes, diced (about 3 cups, or 540 g)

1 tablespoon AR's Hot Southern Honey (mild or hot)

½ teaspoon smoked paprika

½ teaspoon kosher salt

¼ teaspoon freshly ground black pepper

¼ cup (60 ml) heavy whipping cream

1¼ pounds (560 g) 26–30 count shrimp, peeled and deveined

2 tablespoons fresh lemon juice

3 scallions, chopped, for serving

1 tablespoon chopped fresh flat-leaf parsley, for serving

1. To make the grits: Bring the water to a boil in a medium saucepan over medium-high heat. Add the grits while whisking constantly to avoid lumps. Reduce the heat to low and simmer for 25 to 30 minutes, whisking often, until the grits are tender. Whisk in the 2 tablespoons butter, 1 tablespoon hot honey, and 1 teaspoon salt.

2. While the grits cook, make the shrimp: Melt the 1 tablespoon butter in a medium skillet over medium-high heat. Add the garlic and cook for 30 seconds, stirring, until fragrant but not browned. Add the tomatoes and any juices, 1 tablespoon hot honey, paprika, ½ teaspoon salt, and pepper. Let the mixture come to a boil, then reduce the heat so that the sauce simmers. Simmer for 8 to 10 minutes, until the sauce starts to thicken. Add the cream and simmer for 2 minutes more.

3. Add the shrimp to the sauce and gently simmer for about 4 minutes, or until the shrimp are pink and starting to curl. Stir in the lemon juice.

4. Divide the grits among bowls and spoon on the shrimp and sauce. Top with the chopped scallions and parsley.

Black Pepper Tofu

30 minutes *Serves 4*

1 (14-ounce, or 400-g) block firm tofu, drained

¼ cup (60 ml) extra-virgin olive oil, plus more for cooking the tofu

¾ cup (100 g) cornstarch

3 shallots, thinly sliced

2 cloves garlic, finely chopped

1 tablespoon grated ginger

6 tablespoons less-sodium soy sauce

¼ cup (60 ml) water

2 tablespoons AR's Hot Southern Honey (mild or hot)

2 tablespoons barbecue sauce

1 tablespoon coarsely ground black pepper

3 scallions (white and light green parts), thinly sliced, for serving

1 tablespoon toasted sesame seeds, for serving

1. Pat the tofu dry and cut into 1-inch (2.5 cm) cubes.

2. Heat about ¼ inch (6 mm) of oil in a large nonstick skillet over medium-high heat. Line a plate with two paper towels and set aside.

3. In a medium bowl, toss together the tofu and cornstarch to lightly coat.

4. Add the tofu to the hot oil and cook for 7 to 8 minutes, turning halfway through, until golden brown and crisp. Transfer to the prepared plate and set aside.

5. Pour the oil out of the skillet and wipe clean with a paper towel. Return the skillet to medium heat and add the ¼ cup (60 ml) oil. Add the shallots, garlic, and ginger and cook, stirring occasionally, for 12 to 15 minutes, until the shallots are very soft, reducing the heat as necessary to prevent scorching.

6. In a small bowl, whisk together the soy sauce, water, hot honey, barbecue sauce, and pepper.

7. Add the tofu to the skillet and, using a spatula, turn to coat with the shallot mixture. Add the soy sauce mixture and let simmer, stirring the tofu, for about 2 minutes, or until the sauce starts to thicken.

8. Sprinkle with the sliced scallions and sesame seeds. Serve immediately.

Sausage and Pepper Pizza

45 minutes *Serves 4*

Pizza

1 pound (454 g) homemade or store-bought pizza dough, at room temperature

All-purpose flour, for dusting

8 ounces (227 g) Italian sausage, casings removed

½ teaspoon fennel seeds, crushed

Extra-virgin olive oil, for the pan

6 ounces (170 g) fresh mozzarella, sliced

1 small red bell pepper, very thinly sliced

½ small red onion, very thinly sliced

¼ cup (25 g) grated Parmesan

AR's Hot Southern Honey (mild or hot), for drizzling

Sauce

1 (28-ounce, or 794-g) can plum tomatoes

2 tablespoons extra-virgin olive oil

2 cloves garlic, grated

1 teaspoon dried oregano

½ teaspoon kosher salt

¼ teaspoon freshly ground black pepper

Pinch of sugar

1. Preheat the oven to 500°F (260°C; gas mark 10).

2. To make the pizza: Cut the pizza dough in half and shape into two balls. Lightly dust with flour, cover with a clean dish towel, and let rest on the counter.

3. To make the sauce: Lift the tomatoes out of their juice (save the juice for another use) and add to a blender. Add the 2 tablespoons oil, garlic, oregano, salt, pepper, and sugar. Blend until the tomatoes are chopped but not completely pureed.

4. Pour the sauce into a medium saucepan over medium heat. Simmer for about 10 minutes, or until slightly thickened.

5. Cook the sausage in a medium skillet over medium-high heat, crumbling it into small pieces with a wooden spoon as it cooks, for 6 to 7 minutes, until cooked through. Stir in the crushed fennel seeds and remove from the heat.

6. Lightly oil a large sheet pan. Shape each dough ball into a 10-inch (25 cm) roundish disk. Place on the prepared pan.

7. For each pizza, spread 3 to 4 tablespoons of sauce, leaving a ½-inch (1 cm) border (save the remaining sauce for another pizza night). Dividing evenly, lay the slices of mozzarella over the sauce. Add the bell pepper, onion, and sausage. Sprinkle with the Parmesan.

8. Bake the pizzas for 15 to 18 minutes, until the crust is golden brown and crisp.

9. Drizzle with hot honey and serve.

Roasted Sweet Potato and Corn Tacos

35 minutes *Serves 4*

1¼ pounds (560 g) sweet potatoes, cut into ½-inch (1 cm) dice

2 large poblano peppers, seeded and cut crosswise into ½-inch-thick (1 cm) strips

1 cup (145 g) fresh corn kernels

3 tablespoons extra-virgin olive oil, plus more for frying

3 tablespoons AR's Hot Southern Honey (mild or hot)

¾ teaspoon kosher salt

¼ teaspoon freshly ground black pepper

⅛ to ¼ teaspoon chipotle powder

8 corn tortillas

Canola or grapeseed oil, for frying

1 avocado, sliced

Fresh cilantro, for serving

Hot sauce (such as AR's Peach Hot Sauce), for serving

1. Preheat the oven to 425°F (220°C; gas mark 7).

2. On a large rimmed sheet pan, combine the sweet potatoes, poblanos, and corn.

3. In a small bowl, whisk together the olive oil, hot honey, salt, black pepper, and chipotle powder. Pour over the sweet potato mixture and, using your hands, toss to coat. Spread into a single layer.

4. Roast for 25 to 30 minutes, stirring halfway through, until the sweet potatoes are tender and caramelized around the edges.

5. Heat about ¼ inch (6 mm) of canola oil in a small skillet over medium-high heat. Line a plate with two paper towels and set aside.

6. Fry the tortillas one at a time for about 2 minutes, folding them in half halfway through, flipping as necessary, until crisp but still bendable. Transfer to the prepared plate.

7. Fill the tortillas with the sweet potato mixture, avocado slices, and cilantro. Serve with hot sauce.

Broiled Barbecue Salmon with Dill Cucumbers

40 minutes | *Serves 4*

Salmon

¼ cup (85 g) AR's Hot Southern Honey (mild or hot)

¼ cup (65 g) barbecue sauce

2 tablespoons less-sodium soy sauce

4 (6-ounce, or 170-g) fillets salmon

¼ teaspoon kosher salt

Dill Cucumbers

2 tablespoons AR's Hot Southern Honey (mild or hot)

2 tablespoons white wine vinegar

¼ teaspoon kosher salt

2 cucumbers, peeled and thinly sliced into rounds

1 tablespoon chopped fresh dill

1. To make the salmon: In a small bowl, stir together the ¼ cup (85 g) hot honey, barbecue sauce, and soy sauce. Reserve ¼ cup (60 ml) of the marinade for broiling.
2. Put the salmon in a glass or ceramic baking dish or in a resealable plastic bag. Pour in all but the ¼ cup (60 ml) of the marinade. Coat evenly. Refrigerate for 30 minutes.
3. Meanwhile, make the dill cucumbers: In a medium bowl, whisk together the 2 tablespoons hot honey, vinegar, and salt. Add the cucumbers and dill. Toss well and set aside.
4. Position the oven rack 6 inches (15 cm) from the top. Preheat the broiler to high. Line a sheet pan with foil.
5. Put the salmon fillets on the prepared pan and sprinkle with the salt. Broil for 5 minutes, then spoon on some of the reserved marinade over the tops. Broil for 1 minute, then spoon on the remaining marinade. Broil for 1 to 2 minutes more, until the tops are caramelized and the salmon is opaque throughout.
6. Serve the salmon with the dill cucumbers.

Grilled Chipotle Chicken Cobb Salad with Candied Bacon

55 minutes *Serves 4 to 6*

Salad

2 tablespoons extra-virgin olive oil

2 cloves garlic, finely chopped

½ teaspoon chipotle powder

½ teaspoon kosher salt

⅛ teaspoon freshly ground black pepper

2 (8-ounce, or 225-g) boneless, skinless chicken breasts

8 slices bacon

AR's Hot Southern Honey (mild or hot), for drizzling

3 hearts of romaine lettuce, coarsely chopped

4 large hard-boiled eggs, sliced

1 cup (150 g) cherry tomatoes, halved

1 cucumber, quartered lengthwise and sliced

1 avocado, diced

4 ounces (113 g) blue cheese, crumbled (1 cup)

12 fresh chive stalks

Vinaigrette

2 tablespoons red wine vinegar

2 teaspoons AR's Hot Southern Honey (mild or hot)

1½ teaspoons Dijon mustard

½ teaspoon kosher salt

¼ teaspoon freshly ground black pepper

¼ cup (60 ml) extra-virgin olive oil

1. To make the salad: In a medium bowl, combine the oil, garlic, chipotle powder, ½ teaspoon salt, and ⅛ teaspoon pepper. Add the chicken breasts and turn to coat. Cover and let marinate for at least 30 minutes or overnight in the refrigerator.

2. Preheat the grill to medium.

3. Grill the chicken for 6 to 7 minutes per side, until cooked through. Let rest before slicing into ¼-inch-thick (6 mm) pieces.

4. Preheat the oven to 400°F (205°C; gas mark 6).

5. For the bacon, line a rimmed sheet pan with parchment paper and place an oven-safe wire rack in the pan. Arrange the bacon in a single layer on the rack. Bake for 10 minutes. Then drizzle some hot honey over each slice of bacon. Bake for 8 to 10 minutes more, until the bacon is crisp (bake longer if using thick bacon). It will crisp up more as it cools.

6. To make the vinaigrette: In a small bowl, whisk together the vinegar, 2 teaspoons hot honey, mustard, ½ teaspoon salt, and ¼ teaspoon pepper. Whisk in the oil until emulsified.

7. To assemble the salad, first make a bed of lettuce on a large platter and drizzle with some of the vinaigrette. Arrange the hard-boiled eggs, tomatoes, cucumber, avocado, blue cheese, and chicken in rows atop the lettuce. Crumble the bacon over the top.

8. Use kitchen scissors to snip the chives into small pieces over the salad. Drizzle with more of the vinaigrette and serve.

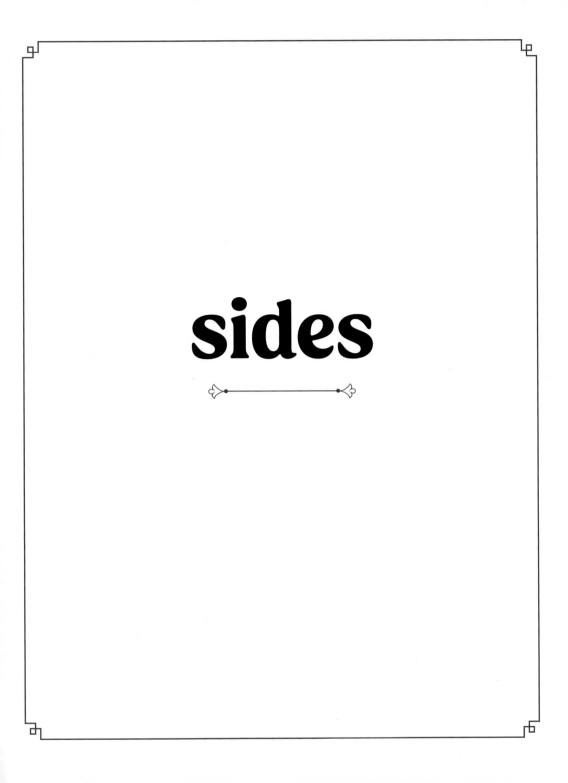

sides

Fried Green Tomatoes
with Smoky Remoulade

30 minutes *Serves 4 to 6*

Fried Green Tomatoes

1 cup (240 ml) buttermilk

2 tablespoons AR's Hot Southern Honey (mild or hot), plus more for drizzling

2 pounds (907 g) medium green tomatoes (about 4), sliced into ½-inch-thick (1 cm) rounds

1½ cups (210 g) finely ground cornmeal

½ cup (60 g) all-purpose flour

1 teaspoon kosher salt

Extra-virgin olive oil, for frying

Smoky Remoulade

1 cup (227 g) mayonnaise

½ cup (68 g) chopped dill pickles

2 tablespoons chopped fresh flat-leaf parsley

2 tablespoons ketchup

2 tablespoons fresh lemon juice

1 tablespoon hot sauce (such as Tabasco)

¾ teaspoon onion powder

½ teaspoon smoked paprika

¼ teaspoon kosher salt

⅛ teaspoon cayenne pepper (optional)

1. To make the fried green tomatoes: In a large baking dish, whisk together the buttermilk and hot honey. Add the tomatoes, turning them to coat, and let marinate for 20 minutes.

2. To make the smoky remoulade: In a small bowl, stir together the mayonnaise, pickles, parsley, ketchup, lemon juice, hot sauce, onion powder, paprika, ¼ teaspoon salt, and cayenne pepper (if using). Refrigerate while you fry the tomatoes.

3. In a shallow bowl, combine the cornmeal, flour, and 1 teaspoon salt. One at a time, evenly coat the tomatoes in the cornmeal mixture and place on a clean plate.

4. In a large skillet, heat about ¼ inch (6 mm) of oil over medium-high heat. Line a plate with two paper towels and set aside.

5. To test if the oil is hot, add a little cornmeal mixture to the oil. It should sizzle immediately. Cooking in batches and without overcrowding the skillet, fry the tomatoes for 2 to 3 minutes per side, until golden brown and crisp. Transfer to the prepared plate.

6. Drizzle the fried green tomatoes with hot honey and serve with the remoulade. Serve immediately.

Hot Honey and Cumin–Roasted Carrots

40 minutes *Serves 4*

1¼ pounds (560 g) thin carrots (or thick carrots, quartered lengthwise)

2 tablespoons extra-virgin olive oil

½ teaspoon ground cumin

½ teaspoon kosher salt

¼ teaspoon freshly ground black pepper

2 tablespoons AR's Hot Southern Honey (mild or hot)

Chopped fresh herbs (such as parsley, cilantro, or dill), for serving (optional)

1. Preheat the oven to 425°F (220°C; gas mark 7).

2. On a rimmed sheet pan, toss together the carrots and oil. Sprinkle with the cumin, salt, and pepper and toss again. Spread into a single layer.

3. Roast for 20 minutes, then give the carrots a shake. Roast for 5 minutes more, then drizzle with the hot honey. Roast for 5 to 10 minutes more, until nice and caramelized.

4. Serve the carrots topped with fresh herbs (if using), but they are also delicious on their own.

Collard Greens with Caramelized Onions and Bacon

40 minutes *Serves 4*

8 ounces (227 g) bacon, cut crosswise into ½-inch (1 cm) pieces

1 large yellow onion, sliced

½ teaspoon kosher salt, divided, plus more for the water and to taste

1 large bunch collard greens, stemmed and leaves cut into large, bite-size pieces

2 tablespoons AR's Hot Southern Honey (mild or hot)

3 tablespoons apple cider vinegar

¼ teaspoon freshly ground black pepper

1. In a large skillet over medium-high heat, cook the bacon for 7 to 8 minutes, until crisp. Pour off all but 2 tablespoons of the fat.

2. Add the onion and ¼ teaspoon of the salt to the skillet with the bacon. Cook for 20 to 25 minutes, stirring often, until the onion is caramelized. Reduce the heat if the mixture starts to scorch.

3. While the bacon-onion mixture cooks, bring a large pot of water to a boil and salt it. Add the collard greens and cook for about 5 minutes, or until tender, then drain.

4. Stir the hot honey into the bacon-onion mixture, then stir in the vinegar. Stir in the collard greens.

5. Season with the pepper and the remaining ¼ teaspoon salt. Taste for salt; you may want to add a little more. Serve hot.

Charred Hot Honey Corn

6 ears corn, shucked

1 tablespoon extra-virgin olive oil

¼ cup (½ stick, or 60 g) unsalted butter

1 tablespoon AR's Hot Southern Honey (mild or hot)

2 scallions (white and light green parts), thinly sliced, plus more for serving

½ jalapeño pepper, chopped

½ teaspoon chili powder

½ teaspoon kosher salt, plus more to taste

¼ teaspoon freshly ground pepper

Cotija cheese, crumbled, for serving (optional)

1. Preheat the grill to medium-high.

2. Drizzle the ears of corn with the oil and rub to coat.

3. Grill the corn for 10 to 12 minutes, turning occasionally, until charred. When the corn is cool enough to handle, cut the kernels from the cobs.

4. In a medium skillet, add the butter, hot honey, scallions, jalapeño, chili powder, salt, and pepper. Turn on the heat to medium and stir everything together until well combined. Once the mixture starts to bubble, stir in the corn kernels. Cook for about 1 minute, or until heated through. Taste for salt; you may want to add a little more.

5. Serve the corn topped with the cheese (if using) and some more sliced scallions.

Tomato and Cucumber Salad with Grilled Halloumi and Bread

20 minutes *Serves 4*

1½ pounds (680 g) beefsteak tomatoes (about 3 medium tomatoes), cored and cut into ¾-inch-thick (2 cm) wedges

1 cucumber, peeled, halved lengthwise, and sliced into ¼-inch-thick (6 mm) half-moons.

½ medium red onion, very thinly sliced

3 tablespoons extra-virgin olive oil, plus more for grilling

1½ tablespoons red wine vinegar

¾ teaspoon flaky sea salt (or ½ teaspoon kosher salt)

½ teaspoon dried oregano

¼ teaspoon freshly ground black pepper

4 slices crusty bread, cut 1 inch (2.5 cm) thick

12 ounces (340 g) halloumi cheese

AR's Hot Southern Honey (mild or hot), for drizzling

1. Preheat the grill to medium-high.

2. In a large bowl, combine the tomatoes, cucumber, and onion. Drizzle in the oil and vinegar, then sprinkle with the salt, oregano, and pepper. Let marinate while you grill the bread and halloumi.

3. Drizzle both sides of the bread slices with some oil. Grill for 1 to 2 minutes per side, until crisp and dark grill marks have formed.

4. Slice the halloumi into scant ½-inch-thick (1 cm) slices. Pat dry. Lightly coat the slices with a little oil.

5. Oil the grill grates and grill the halloumi for about 1 minute per side, or until grill marks form.

6. Cut the grilled bread into bite-size cubes. Add to the salad and toss.

7. Divide the salad among bowls.

8. Drizzle the halloumi with a generous amount of hot honey and place a couple of slices on each salad.

Cornbread with Hot Honey Butter

35 minutes *Serves 6 to 8*

Cornbread

1½ cups (210 g) finely
ground cornmeal

½ cup (60 g) all-purpose flour

1 teaspoon kosher salt

1 teaspoon baking powder

½ teaspoon baking soda

½ cup plus 3 tablespoons (165 g)
unsalted butter

2 large eggs

1½ cups (350 ml) buttermilk

3 tablespoons AR's Hot Southern
Honey (mild or hot), plus more
for drizzling

Honey Butter

½ cup (120 g) unsalted butter,
at room temperature

3 tablespoons AR's Hot Southern
Honey (mild or hot)

½ teaspoon kosher salt

1. Preheat the oven to 425°F (220°C; gas mark 7). Place a 9- to 10-inch
(23 to 25 cm) cast-iron skillet in the oven while it preheats to get the
skillet nice and hot.

2. To make the cornbread: In a large bowl, whisk together the cornmeal,
flour, 1 teaspoon salt, baking powder, and baking soda.

3. Take the skillet out of the oven and add the ½ cup plus 3 tablespoons
(165 g) butter to it. It will melt quickly; it's even better if the butter gets
a little browned.

4. In a medium bowl, whisk together the eggs, then whisk in the buttermilk
and 3 tablespoons hot honey. Whisk in the melted butter, leaving a nice
coating of butter in the skillet.

5. Stir the wet ingredients into the dry ingredients; do not overmix.

6. Pour the batter into the hot skillet. Bake for about 20 minutes, or until a toothpick inserted in the middle comes out clean. Remove from the oven. Drizzle a little more hot honey over the cornbread and brush to evenly coat the top.

7. While the cornbread bakes, make the honey butter: In a small bowl, stir together the ½ cup (120 g) butter, 3 tablespoons hot honey, and ½ teaspoon salt until well combined.

8. Serve the honey butter with the warm cornbread.

Green Beans with Hot Honey Almonds

20 minutes *Serves 4 to 6*

¼ teaspoon kosher salt, plus more for the water and to taste

1 pound (454 g) fresh green beans, trimmed

3 tablespoons extra-virgin olive oil

½ cup (45 g) sliced almonds

2 tablespoons AR's Hot Southern Honey (mild or hot)

¼ teaspoon freshly ground black pepper

1 lemon, for zesting

1. Bring a large pot of water to a boil, then salt it.

2. Add the green beans to the pot. Once the water comes back to a boil, cook the beans for 3 to 5 minutes, until just tender. Transfer them to a large bowl of ice water to stop the cooking process and preserve their color. Drain the beans and pat dry with a paper towel.

3. In a medium skillet, heat the oil over medium heat. Add the almonds and cook for 2 to 3 minutes, stirring often, until they are golden brown.

4. Stir in the hot honey, ¼ teaspoon salt, and pepper. Add the beans and stir to coat.

5. Grate in the zest from half of the lemon. Stir the beans once more.

6. Taste for salt; you may want to add a pinch more. Serve immediately.

Melon and Grapefruit Salad with Walnuts and Blue Cheese

20 minutes *Serves 4*

Salad

1 cup (100 g) walnuts

1 large grapefruit

1 large head butter lettuce, torn

3 cups (465 g) bite-size melon pieces (such as watermelon, cantaloupe, or honeydew)

4 ounces (140 g) blue cheese, crumbled (1 cup)

Vinaigrette

1 shallot, finely chopped

2 tablespoons white wine vinegar

2 tablespoons AR's Hot Southern Honey (mild or hot)

2 tablespoons reserved grapefruit juice

¼ cup (60 ml) extra-virgin olive oil

¾ teaspoon kosher salt

¼ teaspoon freshly ground black pepper

1. Preheat the oven to 350°F (175°C; gas mark 4).

2. To make the salad: Spread the walnuts on a rimmed sheet pan and bake for 8 to 10 minutes, until toasted and fragrant.

3. Section the grapefruit. Squeeze out 2 tablespoons of juice from the remaining membranes for the vinaigrette.

4. To assemble the salads, dividing evenly among bowls, make beds with the lettuce and top with melon pieces, blue cheese, walnuts, and grapefruit sections.

5. To make the vinaigrette: In a small bowl, whisk together the shallot, vinegar, hot honey, reserved grapefruit juice, oil, salt, and pepper.

6. Drizzle the dressing over the salads.

Arugula Salad with Shaved Parmesan, Toasted Pine Nuts, and Truffle Salt

CONTRIBUTED BY LIZI HEAPS

5 minutes ❖ *Serves 4*

¼ cup (60 ml) extra-virgin olive oil

⅓ cup (50 g) pine nuts

Truffle salt, to taste

Juice of 1 lemon

5 cups (100 g) baby arugula

Parmesan shavings, to taste

AR's Hot Southern Honey (mild or hot), for drizzling

1. In a small shallow saucepan, heat the olive oil over low heat. Add the pine nuts, stirring to lightly toast them, about 2 minutes. Remove from heat when they are light brown. Lightly salt with truffle salt, then add the fresh lemon juice. Stir to combine.
2. In an 11-inch (28 cm) round shallow dish, lay down a bed of arugula, sprinkle with the Parmesan shavings, top with the toasted pine nuts, and season with a little more truffle salt. Mix everything together.
3. Drizzle the salad with hot honey and serve immediately.

Sweet Heat Baked Beans

3 hours or overnight (depending on bean-soaking method)   Serves 8

---

1 pound (454 g) dried navy beans, rinsed (if you prefer to use canned beans, see Note on page 104)

1 bay leaf

2 cloves garlic

1 tablespoon plus ¼ teaspoon kosher salt, divided, plus more to taste

4 ounces (115 g) bacon, cut crosswise into ½-inch (1 cm) pieces

1 large yellow onion, chopped

¼ cup (60 g) ketchup

¼ cup (85 g) AR's Hot Southern Honey (mild or hot)

2 tablespoons (40 g) unsulfured molasses

1 tablespoon (30 ml) apple cider vinegar

2 teaspoons Worcestershire sauce

1 teaspoon ground mustard

½ teaspoon smoked paprika

½ teaspoon freshly ground black pepper

---

1. To soak the beans overnight, put them in a large bowl and cover with cold water by 2 inches (5 cm). Stir in 1 tablespoon of the salt and refrigerate. Alternatively, you can do a quick soak. In a large pot, combine the beans and 1 tablespoon of the salt. Add cold water to cover by 2 inches (5 cm) and place over medium-high heat. Let come to a boil, then remove from the heat and let stand for 1 hour.

2. Drain the soaked beans and rinse. Put them in a large pot and cover with cold water by 3 inches (7.5 cm). Add the bay leaf, garlic, and remaining ¼ teaspoon salt. Place over medium-high heat and let come to a boil. Partially cover the pot with a lid and reduce the heat so that the beans simmer gently. Cook the beans, stirring occasionally, for 1 to 2 hours, or until tender (the age of the bean will determine the cooking time). Be sure to check that the beans remain covered by water while cooking, adding

more water if necessary. Remove the pot from the heat and let the beans cool to room temperature in their cooking liquid. Drain the beans and reserve the cooking liquid. Discard the bay leaf.

3. While the beans cool, cook the bacon in a large pot (preferably a Dutch oven) over medium-high heat for 6 to 7 minutes, until crisp. Add the onion and cook, stirring occasionally, for 10 to 12 minutes, until the onion is very tender. Remove from the heat.

(continued on page 104)

(continued from page 103)

4. In a small bowl, stir together the ketchup, hot honey, molasses, vinegar, Worcestershire sauce, mustard, paprika, and pepper.

5. Preheat the oven to 325°F (160°C; gas mark 3).

6. Add the cooked beans to the bacon-onion mixture in the pot, then add the ketchup mixture and stir together. Add enough of the reserved cooking liquid from the beans so that it just reaches the surface of the beans (about 1 cup, or 240 ml).

7. Place the pot over medium-high heat and let come to a boil.

8. Transfer the pot to the oven and bake, uncovered, for about 45 minutes, or until the top is caramelized. Let rest for 10 minutes to give the sauce a chance to thicken. Stir once, then serve.

NOTE: If you prefer to use canned beans, drain and rinse three 15-ounce (425 g) cans of navy beans. Add them to the bacon-onion mixture in step 6, then stir in the ketchup mixture. Add enough water so it just reaches the surface of the beans (about 1 cup, or 240 ml) and let come to a boil over medium-high heat. Bake as directed in step 8.

Roasted Acorn Squash with Sage Brown Butter

45 minutes ❈ *Serves 4*

1 acorn squash (about 2¼ pounds, or 1 kg)

2 tablespoons extra-virgin olive oil

½ teaspoon kosher salt, divided

¼ teaspoon freshly ground black pepper

¼ cup (½ stick, or 60 g) unsalted butter

4 cloves garlic, thinly sliced

16 leaves fresh sage

2 tablespoons AR's Hot Southern Honey (mild or hot)

¼ teaspoon kosher salt

1. Preheat the oven to 425°F (220°C; gas mark 7).

2. Cut the squash in half lengthwise and scoop out the seeds. Cut the squash halves into 2-inch-thick (5 cm) wedges. Place the wedges on a rimmed sheet pan, drizzle with the oil, and sprinkle with ¼ teaspoon of the salt and the pepper. Using your hands, toss the squash to evenly coat in the oil. Lay them on their cut sides.

3. Roast for 20 to 25 minutes, until the undersides are golden brown. Flip the squash and roast for about 20 minutes more, or until the other sides are golden brown. Transfer to a serving platter.

4. Melt the butter in a medium skillet over medium heat. Add the garlic and cook for 3 to 5 minutes, swirling the skillet often, until the garlic and butter start to turn golden brown.

5. Add the sage and cook, stirring, for 30 seconds, until crisp. Remove the skillet from the heat and stir in the hot honey and remaining ¼ teaspoon salt.

6. Spoon the sage brown butter over the roasted squash and serve.

Hot Honey Focaccia

30 minutes, plus 14 to 20 hours rising and proofing time ❖ *Serves 8*

1½ cups (350 ml) lukewarm water

1 teaspoon AR's Hot Southern Honey (mild or hot), plus more for drizzling

¼ teaspoon active dry yeast

3¼ cups (390 g) all-purpose flour, plus more for fingertips

1 tablespoon kosher salt

¼ cup (60 ml) extra-virgin olive oil, divided

Flaky sea salt, for sprinkling

1. In a large bowl, whisk together the water, hot honey, and yeast.

2. In a medium bowl, whisk together the flour and kosher salt.

3. Pour the dry mixture into the wet mixture. With a wooden spoon or your hands, mix thoroughly until no dry flour remains. Cover tightly with plastic wrap. Let rise for 12 to 18 hours in the warmest part of your kitchen, until it has more than doubled in volume. It will be very bubbly.

4. Coat the bottom of a 9 × 13-inch (23 × 33 cm) baking pan with 2 tablespoons of the oil.

5. Using floured fingertips, release the dough from the sides of the bowl and gently fold the dough over itself. Pour the dough (it will be very soft) into the prepared pan. Drizzle the remaining 2 tablespoons oil over the dough and lightly rub the oil to coat the top. Gently stretch the dough as best you can to cover the bottom of the pan (probably no more than two-thirds of the pan). Don't force it; the gluten will resist you. Cover tightly with plastic wrap and let rise for about 2 hours, or until doubled (the dough will spread out and fill the pan).

6. Thirty minutes before the dough is done rising, preheat the oven (with the oven rack in the middle) to 500°F (260°C; gas mark 10). If you have a pizza stone, place it on the middle rack.

7. Using your fingertips, gently dimple the dough to make small indentations. Sprinkle with a little flaky sea salt.

8. Slide the pan directly onto the middle rack or onto the pizza stone and bake for 17 to 24 minutes, until golden brown and crisp around the edges. Remove from the pan and let the focaccia cool for 10 minutes on a wire cooling rack.

9. Slice and drizzle with hot honey.

Coleslaw with a Kick

15 minutes *Serves 4 to 6*

8 cups (560 g) shredded green cabbage (about ½ of a large head)

¾ cup (90 g) grated carrot (about 1 large carrot)

½ medium sweet onion, very thinly sliced

2 tablespoons chopped fresh flat-leaf parsley

¾ cup (175 g) mayonnaise

2 tablespoons apple cider vinegar

2 tablespoons white wine vinegar

1½ tablespoons AR's Hot Southern Honey (mild or hot)

2 teaspoons whole-grain mustard

½ teaspoon celery seeds

½ teaspoon kosher salt

¼ teaspoon freshly ground black pepper

1. In a large bowl, toss together the cabbage, carrot, onion, and parsley.

2. In a small bowl, stir together the mayonnaise, apple cider vinegar, white wine vinegar, hot honey, mustard, celery seeds, salt, and pepper.

3. Pour the dressing over the cabbage mixture and toss until well coated.

4. Serve the coleslaw immediately, or make it up to a day in advance, cover, and refrigerate.

desserts

Grilled Pineapple with Coconut Sorbet and Lime

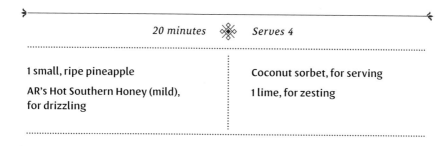

20 minutes ❈ *Serves 4*

1 small, ripe pineapple

AR's Hot Southern Honey (mild),
for drizzling

Coconut sorbet, for serving

1 lime, for zesting

1. Preheat the grill to medium-high.

2. Trim the top and bottom from the pineapple and cut away the skin. Cut the pineapple into four ¾-inch-thick (2 cm) rounds. Put them in a baking dish and lightly drizzle both sides with hot honey.

3. Grill the pineapple rounds for about 2 minutes per side, or until grill marks form. Drizzle the tops with honey, flip, and grill until the honey starts to char. Repeat drizzling and flipping several times until a nice honey crust forms, about 10 minutes total.

4. Divide the pineapple among bowls and add a scoop of sorbet to each. Grate fresh lime zest over the tops.

Hot Honey S'more Brownies

CONTRIBUTED BY ANDRÉA JOHNSON

50 minutes *Serves 9*

Crust

¼ teaspoon salt

½ cup (100 g) granulated sugar

1¼ cups (150 g) graham cracker crumbs

½ cup butter (1 stick, or 120 g), melted

Brownies

2¼ teaspoons vegetable oil

1 tablespoon vanilla extract

2 large eggs

½ cup unsalted butter (1 stick, or 120 g), melted and cooled

¾ cup (75 g) cocoa powder

1¼ cups (250 g) granulated sugar

½ cup (100 g) light brown sugar

½ teaspoon salt

¾ cup plus 4 teaspoons (100 g) all-purpose flour

AR's Hot Southern Honey (mild or hot), for drizzling

1 cup (45 g) mini marshmallows

Flaky sea salt, for topping

---

1. Preheat the oven to 350°F (175°C; gas mark 4). Line an 8 × 8-inch (20 × 20 cm) square baking pan with parchment paper.

2. To make the crust: In a large bowl, combine the ¼ teaspoon salt, 1 cup (100 g) granulated sugar, and graham cracker crumbs. Add the ½ cup (120 g) melted butter, mixing until the mixture is moistened and resembles wet sand. Pour the mixture into the prepared pan and press with your fingers to pack it into the bottom of the pan.

3. To make the brownies: In a medium bowl, add the oil, vanilla, and eggs to the melted and cooled ½ cup butter (120 g).

4. In a large bowl, whisk together the cocoa powder, 1¼ cups (250 g) granulated sugar, brown sugar, ½ teaspoon salt, and flour to combine well.

5. Add the wet ingredients to the dry ingredients and stir until just combined. The mixture will be thick. Pour the brownie batter over the graham cracker

crust in the pan, using a spatula or spoon to spread. Drizzle hot honey on top of the batter and swirl with a toothpick.

6. Bake for 35 minutes, or until a skewer inserted into the center comes out mostly dry with a few crumbs. Remove from the oven and place the marshmallows on top of the brownies, allowing the residual heat to melt them. (If desired, using a kitchen torch, carefully toast the marshmallows at this point.) Sprinkle the sea salt on top of the melted marshmallows.

7. Let the brownies cool completely in the pan before cutting and serving. Drizzle with more hot honey, if you like.

Almond Bars

1 hour *Makes 16 bars*

Crust

Nonstick vegetable oil cooking spray, for the pan

1½ cups (180 g) all-purpose flour

⅓ cup (70 g) sugar

½ teaspoon kosher salt

10 or 11 tablespoons cold unsalted butter, cut into small pieces

Filling

½ cup (120 ml) heavy cream

½ cup (170 g) AR's Hot Southern Honey (mild)

¼ cup (50 g) sugar

⅛ teaspoon kosher salt

1¼ cups (115 g) sliced almonds

1. Preheat the oven to 375°F (190°C; gas mark 5). Spray an 8 × 8-inch (20 × 20 cm) square baking pan with cooking spray. Line the bottom of the pan with parchment paper, leaving an overhang on the two opposite sides (for easy lifting once the bars are baked). Set aside.

2. To make the crust: In a food processor, combine the flour, ⅓ cup sugar, ½ teaspoon salt, and 10 tablespoons of the butter. Pulse several times until moist crumbs form and the dough holds together when pinched. If it is a little too dry and not holding together, add the remaining 1 tablespoon butter.

3. Using your fingertips, press the dough evenly over the bottom and ½ inch (1 cm) up the sides of the prepared pan. Bake for 20 to 25 minutes, until light golden brown. If the sides shrink down, gently press them back into shape with a square-edged glass so that the crust still reaches ½ inch (1 cm) up the sides of the pan.

4. While the crust bakes, make the filling: In a small saucepan, combine the cream, hot honey, ¼ cup sugar, and ⅛ teaspoon salt over medium-high heat. Let come to a boil, then reduce the heat to a simmer and cook for 2 minutes. Remove from the heat and stir in the almonds. Pour the filling into the crust, evenly spreading out the sliced almonds.

5. Bake for 25 to 30 minutes, until the sliced almonds are golden brown. Let cool completely before lifting out of the pan and cutting into bars.

Caramel Apples with Vanilla Ice Cream

30 minutes ❈ *Serves 4*

4 crisp medium-size apples (such as Granny Smith)

2 tablespoons, plus ¼ cup (85 g) AR's Hot Southern Honey (mild), divided

2 tablespoons unsalted butter

½ cup (100 g) sugar

Small pinch of kosher salt

Vanilla ice cream, for serving

1. Peel, halve, and core the apples. Put them in a large bowl and toss with 2 tablespoons of the hot honey.

2. Melt the butter in a medium cast-iron or heavy-bottomed skillet over medium heat. Stir in the sugar (it will be crumbly at first). Cook for about 5 minutes, stirring occasionally, until the sugar dissolves and turns a dark caramel color. (Do not touch! It is extremely hot.)

3. Add the remaining ¼ cup (85 g) hot honey and salt to the skillet (it will sizzle). Using tongs, place the apples, cut sides down, in the skillet and pour in any remaining juices. Let them simmer in the caramel for 10 minutes, basting occasionally with a spoon. Flip the apples over and simmer, basting often, for about 10 more minutes, or until the apples are tender and the caramel has thickened. Let the apples cool for a few minutes.

4. Serve the caramel apples in bowls topped with vanilla ice cream.

Stone Fruit Tarts

35 minutes Serves 4

1 sheet frozen puff pastry (at least 9 × 9 inches, or 23 × 23 cm), thawed

½ cup (125 g) fresh ricotta cheese

2 tablespoons AR's Hot Southern Honey (mild), divided, plus more for drizzling

1 lemon, for zesting

½ pound (227 g) stone fruit (such as plums, apricots, peaches, or nectarines)

3 tablespoons apricot preserves

1. Preheat the oven to 400°F (205°C; gas mark 6). Line a sheet pan with parchment paper.

2. Cut the puff pastry sheet into four 4½-inch (11.5 cm) squares. Place on the prepared pan. Using the tip of a paring knife, lightly score a ¾-inch (2 cm) border around each square without cutting through the pastry.

3. In a medium bowl, stir together the ricotta, 1 tablespoon of the honey, and the lemon zest from half of the lemon. Dividing evenly, spread the ricotta mixture within the borders of each puff pastry square.

4. Slice the stone fruit into thin wedges. Lay the fruit over the ricotta mixture.

5. Bake for 20 to 23 minutes, until the puff pastry is golden brown.

6. In a small skillet, combine the apricot preserves and remaining 1 tablespoon honey over medium heat. Let come to a boil. Remove from the heat and brush over the tops of the warm tarts to add flavor and shine.

7. Serve warm or at room temperature with hot honey for drizzling.

Strawberry-Rhubarb Cobbler

1 hour *Serves 6*

Strawberries and Rhubarb

1 pound (454 g) small-medium fresh strawberries, quartered

1 pound (454 g) rhubarb, thinly sliced

½ cup (100 g) sugar

1 tablespoon all-purpose flour

3 tablespoons AR's Hot Southern Honey (mild)

Dough

1½ cups (180 g) all-purpose flour, plus more for work surface

3 tablespoons sugar

2 teaspoons baking powder

½ teaspoon kosher salt

6 tablespoons cold unsalted butter, cut into small pieces

⅔ cup (160 ml) heavy cream, plus more for brushing

1. Preheat the oven to 375°F (190°C; gas mark 5).

2. To prepare the strawberries and rhubarb: In a large bowl, toss together the strawberries, rhubarb, ½ cup sugar, and 1 tablespoon flour. Stir in the hot honey. Pour into a 1½-quart (1.4 L) baking dish. Set aside.

3. To make the dough: In a medium bowl, whisk together the 1½ cups (180 g) flour, 3 tablespoons sugar, baking powder, and salt. Add the butter and, using a pastry cutter or your fingertips, cut the butter into pea-size pieces. Pour in the cream and gently mix with a fork until the dough is moistened.

4. Gently knead the dough to bring it together. On a lightly floured work surface, shape the dough into a ½-inch-thick (1 cm) disk. Using a 2½-inch (6 cm) round cutter or glass, cut out rounds from the dough. Reshape and cut the scraps as necessary.

5. Lay the rounds over the fruit mixture in the baking dish, without overlapping, and brush the tops with a little cream. Place the baking pan on a rimmed sheet pan.

6. Bake for 40 to 45 minutes, until the topping is golden brown and the fruit is bubbling.

7. Serve warm.

Peach Cake

1 hour   *Serves 6*

Nonstick vegetable oil cooking spray, for the pan

4 medium fresh peaches (about 1¼ pounds, or 560 g)

1 tablespoon AR's Hot Southern Honey (mild)

1¼ cups (150 g) all-purpose flour

½ teaspoon baking powder

½ teaspoon baking soda

½ teaspoon kosher salt

½ cup (1 stick, or 120 g) unsalted butter, at room temperature

1 cup (200 g) sugar

2 large eggs

1 teaspoon pure vanilla extract

½ cup (60 ml) buttermilk, at room temperature

Lightly sweetened whipped cream, for serving

1. Preheat the oven to 350°F (175°C; gas mark 4). Spray an 8 × 8-inch (20 × 20 cm) square baking pan with cooking spray. Line the bottom of the pan with parchment paper, leaving an overhang on the two opposite sides (for easy lifting once the cake is baked). Set aside.

2. Peel the peaches. Slice them into ½-inch-thick (1 cm) wedges and add to a small bowl. Toss with the hot honey and let marinate while you make the cake batter.

3. In a small bowl, whisk together the flour, baking powder, baking soda, and salt.

4. In a large bowl using an electric mixer or in the bowl of a stand mixer, beat together the butter and sugar on medium-high speed for 1 to 2 minutes, until fluffy. Add the eggs and vanilla and beat until creamy. On low speed, mix in half of the dry ingredients. Mix in the buttermilk, then the remaining dry ingredients.

5. Scrape the batter into the prepared pan and spread evenly. Place the peaches in a single layer over the batter and drizzle any remaining juices over the top.

6. Bake for 38 to 40 minutes, until a toothpick inserted into the middle comes out with a few moist crumbs attached. Let cool for 20 minutes on a wire cooling rack before lifting the cake out of the pan to cool completely.

7. Serve with whipped cream. (This cake is best the same day it is made.)

cocktails

Going to the Country

CONTRIBUTED BY ELIAS ADAMS

5 minutes ❈ *Serves 1*

1½ ounces (45 ml) tequila (such as Lunazul Reposado Tequila)

¾ ounce (22 ml) Aperol

½ ounce (15 ml) fresh lemon juice

¾ ounce (22 ml) fresh peach juice

¾ ounce (22 ml) AR's Hot Southern Honey (mild or hot)

1 egg white

2 ounces soda water

1 lemon peel twist, for garnishing

Freshly cracked pink pepper, for garnishing

1. Shake the tequila, Aperol, lemon juice, peach juice, hot honey, and egg white in a shaker tin with ice.

2. Strain the liquid back into the shaker tin without ice, and dry shake.

3. Add the soda water to a collins glass and pour the liquid from the shaker tin over the soda water.

4. Garnish with a lemon peel twist and some cracked pink peppercorn.

Mariner's Revenge

CONTRIBUTED BY ELIAS ADAMS

5 minutes ❈ *Serves 1*

1½ ounces (45 ml) rye whiskey (such as Rittenhouse Rye 100)

½ ounce (15 ml) Zucca

½ ounce rum (such as Smith & Cross Traditional Jamaican Rum)

¼ ounce (7.5 ml) AR's Bourbon Barrel Aged Hot-Hot Southern Honey

2 dashes cacao nib tincture (or chocolate bitters)

Orange peel

1. Stir the whiskey, Zucca, rum, bourbon honey, and cacao tincture with ice in a shaker tin.

2. Strain into a coupe glass.

3. Express the oils from the orange peel into the drink and discard.

Keeping in Touch

CONTRIBUTED BY ELIAS ADAMS

5 minutes *Serves 1*

2 ounces (60 ml) dark rum (such as Plantation Original Dark Rum)

½ ounce (15 ml) crème de banana

½ ounce (15 ml) AR's Bourbon Barrel Aged Hot-Hot Southern Honey

½ ounce (15 ml) fresh lemon juice

½ ounce (15 ml) Coco López Cream of Coconut

Crushed ice

½ ounce (15 ml) black tea

1 pineapple leaf, for garnishing

1. Whip shake the rum, crème de banana, bourbon honey, lemon juice, and Coco López with crushed ice in a shaker tin.

2. Strain into a julep glass and top with the black tea.

3. Garnish with the pineapple leaf.

NOTE: For a refreshing mocktail, omit the alcohol and top with seltzer or sparkling water.

That Will Do

CONTRIBUTED BY ELIAS ADAMS

5 minutes ❈ *Serves 1*

2 ounces (60 ml) cognac

¼ ounce (7.5 ml) AR's Hot Southern Honey (mild or hot)

¼ ounce (7.5 ml) chai syrup

2 dashes black walnut bitters

2 dashes Angostura Bitters

1 large ice cube, for serving

1 lemon crown, for garnishing

1. Stir the cognac, hot honey, chai syrup, walnut bitters, and Angostura Bitters with ice in a shaker tin.

2. Strain into a rocks glass over the large ice cube.

3. Garnish with the lemon crown.

Midnight Landing

CONTRIBUTED BY ELIAS ADAMS

5 minutes *Serves 1*

2 ounces (60 ml) bourbon whisky (such as Evan Williams White Label Bottled-in-Bond)

¼ to ½ ounce (7.5 to 15 ml) AR's Southern Wildflower Honey (depending on taste)

½ ounce (15 ml) Amaro Montenegro

¼ ounce (7.5 ml) Galliano

2 dashes orange bitters

1 large ice cube, for serving

1 sprig rosemary, for garnishing

1. Stir the whiskey, honey, Amaro Montenegro, Galliano, and orange bitters with ice in a shaker tin.

2. Strain into a rocks glass over the large ice cube.

3. Garnish with the sprig of rosemary.

Index

About AR's Hot Southern Honey

AR's Hot Southern Honey began in Richmond, Virginia, in 2015 when founder, Ames Russell, dreamed up a method for combining two of his favorite flavors—sweet and spicy—into one scintillating Southern honey.

Their products are available nationwide at small specialty shops, independent grocers, and grocery chains and on their website, Amazon, and other online channels. To learn more about AR's Hot Southern Honey and purchase their products, visit hotsouthernhoney.com.

AR's Hot Southern Honey product lineup:
- Hot-Mild Honey
- Hot-Hot Honey
- Bourbon Barrel Aged Hot-Hot Honey
- Wildflower Honey
- Clover Honey
- Peach Hot Sauce
- Spicy Honey Peanut Butter
- Southern Wildflower Honey Peanut Butter

About Sara Quessenberry

Sara Quessenberry is a cookbook author, food stylist, and recipe developer. She is the co-author of the recent New York Times Best Seller, *Vegan, at Times.* She also collaborated on *The Can't Cook Book* and *Food Swings*, also New York Times Best Sellers. Sara lives in New York City.

About the Recipe Contributors

Elias Adams is the bar manager of Grisette, a French-inspired restaurant located in the Church Hill neighborhood of Richmond, Virginia. Raised in Chesapeake, Virginia, Elias moved to Richmond in 2011 to attend Virginia Commonwealth University. While in school, Elias began his bartending career, in which he discovered his love for the hospitality industry.

Walter Bundy credits his rich culinary heritage from his experiences growing up on the Piankatank River, which is part of the Chesapeake Bay. While attending Hampden-Sydney College, he helped open The Blue Point Restaurant on the Outer Banks of North Carolina, and after graduation, he moved to Santa Fe, New Mexico, where he worked at Mark Miller's Coyote Café. Inspired by the variety of ingredients and flavor profiles unfamiliar to him, Walter enrolled in the New England Culinary Institute, where he completed a degree in Culinary Arts. A desire to learn about wine subsequently led him to Napa Valley, where he worked with renowned chef Thomas Keller at the legendary French Laundry. In May 2001, Walter was named executive chef of Lemaire, a AAA Five Diamond Restaurant, located in the historic Jefferson Hotel in Richmond, Virginia. There, he set the standard for farm-to-table dining. In July 2016, he realized his dream of opening his own restaurant, Shagbark, in Richmond.

Lizi Heaps started as a mother-daughter team when she picked up her mother's brand, The Food Nanny, and took it to a whole new level. Lizi's passion for helping caregivers put meals on the table, especially at dinnertime, launched her success. She spoon-feeds her large Instagram audience fabulous recipes and easy meal plans, along with counseling on portion control while enjoying all varieties of foods. Baking breads is her passion, most notably sourdough, and she shares her love for baking with the ancient grain Kamut. Lizi lives in the mountains of northern Utah with her husband, four children, Jersey cows, chickens, dogs, and cats.

Andréa Johnson is a self-taught baker and confectioner, and owner of Karmalita's Marshmallows & Confections LLC. Her small business in Richmond, Virginia, creates nut-free confections with a focus on leveling up the marshmallow and s'more experience for all ages. Andréa has been featured in many Richmond-area publications and has been lovingly dubbed the "Mallow Queen." She is fast becoming known for her unique flavors and takes on marshmallow confections.

Mike Ledesma is a chef and restauranteur born in Brooklyn, New York, and raised in Baltimore, Maryland. He attended culinary school in Hawaii, where he graduated magna cum laude. Once a financial advisor, he made a career change in 2002, and since moving from the desk to the kitchen, he has worked under "Iron Chef" Roy Yamaguchi and brought his passion for food back to the East Coast, working his way through many favorite Richmond, Virginia, dining establishments. Mike opened his first restaurant, Perch, in 2018, and second restaurant, The Coop, in 2020, both in Richmond. His travels and Filipino heritage continue to inspire his cooking.

Helen Russell has always been passionate about food, thanks to her parents who got her in the kitchen early and shared their food knowledge. She grew up in Richmond, Virginia, and graduated from the University of Alabama, where she majored in hospitality and experienced the business side of the food world. There, she started her Instagram account @dankfood_, where she shares her love for cooking and posts recipes that are delicious and easy to make. Helen continues to pursue her love for food and works for two outstanding chefs in Richmond.